Dyslexia and Stress

Dyslexia and Stress

Edited by T.R. Miles, PhD,
Emeritus Professor of Psychology the University
of Wales, Bangor
and
V.P. Varma, PhD, formerly of the London Institute
of Education

Whurr Publishers Ltd
London

© 1995

First published 1995 by
Whurr Publishers Ltd
19b Compton Terrace, London N1 2UN, England

Reprinted 1997 and 2000

British Library Cataloguing-in-Publication Data
A catalogue record for this book is available from the
British Library.

ISBN 1-897635-22-2

Printed and bound in the UK by Publish on Demand Ltd, London

Foreword

One of the worst aspects of being dyslexic is the vicious circle caused by stress. As soon as I make a mistake I panic, and because I panic I make more mistakes.

In spite of my good fortune in having an interesting and, on the whole, fulfilled working life, there are many days when I feel that I am only just keeping abreast of the stress that is a result of my own inadequacies. For instance, just a simple request such as being asked to write the Foreword to a book, which would be water off a duck's back to many people, fills me with fear. My heart sinks visualising the dozens of versions of the Foreword I shall have to write before I am satisfied, all the time convinced that each version is wrong.

However, I am happy to write the Foreword for this book to share the feelings of frustration and despair that I am sure many of my fellow dyslexics have suffered when doing something as simple as, say, driving a car.

Map-reading, filling out forms, reading aloud, reading road signs are just a few of a long list of things that I find really frustrating. However, with good luck and a great deal of hard work I have managed to master my job.

I remember one experience last summer, which was probably the most frustrating, stressful experience that I have ever had in my whole life.

I was working at the Chichester Festival Theatre in *Relative Values*, and the night before the matinée days I usually stayed in Sussex instead of commuting back to London. On this occasion I was staying with a friend 5 miles outside Chichester, about a 20-minute journey from the theatre. I had been there twice before with my sister, who had helped me find the way, and there had been a full moon so the landmarks were more visible. On this night, however, I was on my own, I was very tired and it was very dark. My first mistake was to turn right instead of left a mile or two after setting out. Eventually, after about 2 hours, I was so lost that I was desperately pounding my fist on the wheel, and even if I did see a signpost I couldn't read it or remember if I had seen it before.

I was so distraught that I was screaming at the top of my voice. I don't ever remember feeling so frustrated, except when I was a child and I was asked to look up words in the dictionary! If I could find the road to London at least I could go home.

I was just turning round, in the hope of finding a hotel, when I saw a signpost to Chichester, but once again I found myself driving up and down an endless series of country lanes, which were even more indistinguishable than the last. About an hour later, tears running down my face and still lost, I saw a young man parking his car, hooted and screeched to a halt to catch him before he disappeared into the night.

'I beg you to help me!', I gasped. 'I'm lost – I've been lost for 3 hours! I'm looking for School Lane and I can't find it.'

'It's there,' he said, calmly pointing into the dark. I couldn't believe it.

Had I not feared I would make a mistake, I'm sure I would not have done so, but I allowed the stress of the situation to get the better of me.

Susan Hampshire

Preface

The literature available on stress in general is extensive (for sources see, in particular, Varma, 1973, 1993) and there is also plenty of evidence from case studies that dyslexics experience more than their fair share of stress (see, for example, Simpson, 1980; Hampshire, 1981; Miles, 1993a, b; Edwards, 1994). As far as we know, however, this is the first book that has attempted to study stress in dyslexia in its own right.

The aim of the book is to increase people's awareness of the stresses that dyslexics undergo and to encourage reflection on ways in which these stresses can be avoided.

There will, of course, be scope in the future for systematic comparisons between dyslexics and non-dyslexics in respect of stress levels, and in particular for the use of physiological measures. Our present purpose, however, is more limited; it is rather that of putting the notion of stress in dyslexia 'on the map' and showing that it is a topic that merits further investigation.

To achieve this we decided that what was needed was a 'personal' approach in which colleagues with experience of dyslexia were asked to contribute chapters. We did not expect them to report systematic experiments but rather to describe the kinds of situation which the dyslexics of their acquaintance regularly found to be stressful. We also thought it important that there should be contributions from people who were themselves dyslexic, because there is clearly no substitute for first-hand experience.

We were extremely pleased when Susan Hampshire agreed to write the Foreword, and we particularly appreciate the way in which she has chosen to share with us the details of a hideously stressful experience which occurred many years after she became famous.

Chapter 1 is a letter from Karen Dodd. Karen is the mother of a dyslexic girl, now at secondary school, and she sets the stage for the rest of the book by calling attention to the appalling stresses that can arise when parents who approach their child's teachers are shown indifference and sometimes downright hostility. We have shortened her letter slightly but otherwise have reproduced it as it was written.

The next chapter, written by Angela Fawcett, contains an account of the struggles – and the later successes – of her son, Matthew, along with some other very telling case studies. Besides being the mother of a dyslexic son, however, Angela is also one of the most prominent dyslexia researchers in the UK, and her work with Dr Rod Nicolson is internationally known. We therefore encouraged her not to limit her contribution to a discussion of individuals but to say something about her own research and in particular about ways in which it might contribute to our understanding of stress.

The next four chapters are arranged on an 'age' basis. Chapter 3, written by Patience Thomson, is entitled 'Stress factors in early education'; in Chapter 4 Steve Chinn and Maryrose Crossman describe their experiences of stress in dyslexic teenagers; in Chapter 5 Dorothy Gilroy writes about stresses among college students; and in Chapter 6 Gerald Hales deals with stresses in the workplace.

Chapter 7, written by Peter Congdon, returns to the issue of stress in children, and indicates some of the problems that can arise in the case of highly gifted dyslexics, whilst in Chapter 8 Roger Saunders straddles the different age levels by writing about stresses within the family. The setting for Roger's work has been in the United States of America, but dyslexia is no respecter of national boundaries and his conclusions are clearly applicable in many different parts of the world.

Chapter 9 is entitled 'The dyslexics speak for themselves'. The contributors are Michael Newby, Joy Aldridge, Brother Matthew Sasse, Sheena Harrison and Janet Coker. We thought it best to record their contributions as they wrote them, rather than attempt to change style, grammar or spelling. We believe that, had we attempted such changes, something of the personality of the writer would have been lost in the process. Our special thanks are due both to them and to Susan Hampshire for their willingness not only to re-live some highly traumatic experiences but to do so via the written word – a task that, as some of them make clear, can itself be extremely stressful.

In the final chapter we attempt as editors to take stock of the book as a whole and to formulate some tentative conclusions.

We should like to end this introduction with a word of warning. As their brief was to deal with stress, the contributors have quite properly spent time calling attention to things that can go wrong. Our worry is that this may present too gloomy a picture! Let it be remembered, then, that things that our contributors claim to have noticed in *some* dyslexics will not necessarily apply to *all* dyslexics; this would be far too pessimistic a conclusion. For example, just because there are dyslexics who, as a result of their dyslexia, do not make friends easily, it would be a serious mistake to jump to the conclusion that no dyslexic ever makes friends easily. What our contributors mention are essentially risks – the dyslexic tends to be at risk more than others to possible sources of stress, and in the interests of realism it was essential in a book of this kind not to minimise these risks. Our main message, nevertheless, is one of optimism: there is ample evidence that in the right environment dyslexics can lead happy and productive lives. It is our belief that with increased public awareness many of the situations that cause them to feel stress can be avoided; indeed, if it had not been so there would have been little point in writing this book.

Tim Miles
Ved Varma
January 1995

References

Edwards J (1994). *The Scars of Dyslexia*. London: Cassell.

Hampshire S (1981). *Susan's Story*. London: Sidgwick & Jackson.

Miles TR (1993a). *Dyslexia: The Pattern of Difficulties*. London: Whurr.

Miles TR (1993b). *Understanding Dyslexia*. Bath: Amethyst Books.

Simpson E (1980). *Reversals. A Personal Account of Victory over Dyslexia*. London: Gollancz.

Varma VP (Ed.) (1973). *Stresses in Children*. London: London University Press.

Varma VP (1993). *Coping With Unhappy Children*. London: Cassell.

Contents

Contributors

Joy Aldridge, MA, AdvDipEd works with young adults having borderline special needs.

Steve Chinn, PhD is Principal of Mark College, Somerset.

Janet Coker is a professional singer.

Peter Congdon, PhD is Director of the Information Centre for Gifted Children in Solihull.

Maryrose Crossman, CertEd is Head of Care at Mark College, Somerset.

Karen Dodd, DipSW is a qualified social worker.

Angela Fawcett, PhD is a dyslexia researcher in the Department of Psychology, University of Sheffield.

Dorothy Gilroy, BA is tutor to the dyslexic students at the University of Wales, Bangor.

Gerald Hales, PhD is Research Fellow, Institute of Educational Technology, The Open University.

Sheena Harrison, BA is a trainee social worker.

Tim Miles, PhD is Professor Emeritus of Psychology, the University of Wales, Bangor.

Michael Newby, CertEd was formerly Head of Science and other departments at a Comprehensive School.

Brother Matthew Sasse, FSC, MA, DipSpLD is a member of a religious order and a teacher of dyslexics.

Roger Saunders, MA, is a clinical psychologist who works in the Baltimore area, USA, and is a Fellow of the Academy of Orton-Gillingham Practitioners and Educators.

Patience Thomson, MA, MEd is Principal of Fairley House School, London.

Ved Varma, PhD was formerly Educational Psychologist at the London Institute of Education.

Acknowledgements

We are grateful to the British Dyslexia Association for permission to reprint Janet Coker's contribution, which also appears in their publication, *Music and Dyslexia* (1992). We are also grateful to Neil Browning and Stephen Cary for their assistance in the preparation of suitable disks.

Convention
Where 'he' and 'his' are used this should be understood to mean individuals of either sex (see also Chapter 8, p. 97).

Chapter 1
Letter from a mother

KAREN DODD

Dear Mr Miles

I realise that something in print is only a possibility, but feel that it would be very beneficial if you could put something in print as I feel that dyslexia is very isolating and that people do not understand the problems involved.

Writing this is difficult, but I will try to give a condensed account of the experiences of my daughter and I. [Margaret] is my second and youngest child. . . Little things began to fit into place after I found that she was dyslexic (i.e. didn't learn to ride a bike until 8 years old). Margaret had a stammer, spoke late and had speech therapy. No sooner had she started full time school, than she was receiving remedial teaching.

. . . At the age of 9 years I couldn't accept that Margaret's school reports were of a bright happy child who works well and tries hard. I saw a T.V. programme discussing dyslexia and . . . arranged a private assessment for her. I spoke to her remedial teacher about this and this is when I first encountered 'the attitude'. Margaret's remedial teacher had been a very nice woman, helpful and approachable who suddenly went beserk, the real Jekyll & Hyde, I couldn't believe the reaction, she made me feel 3" tall.

I had Margaret assessed and she was indeed dyslexic as was my husband. My husband had always considered himself to be illite-rate as he couldn't write at all and had minimal reading skills . . . I gave the [new] school a copy of Margaret's report and I met with her teacher and the headmaster to discuss what help could be given. Again we met 'the attitude'; we felt interfering parents, over-reacting, trying to tell teacher 'experts' their job. I came out near to tears, I was so angry at the way I had been treated. When I pushed the issue with special ed, Margaret was given 1 hour a week for 12 weeks special ed. Moving houses at an important time in her education was blamed and thrown at me.

Initially Margaret was pleased to find out that she was dyslexic. She said, 'I'm not thick am I mum? I'm dyslexic'. Margaret realised she had a special problem and waited for the special help. The help never materialised and Margaret began to get very frustrated as to 'why no one was helping her'. I requested a formal assessment under the education act but was refused. In view of the private assessment I had I felt their refusal unreasonable and began to write and write. I wrote to MP's, Councillors, County Hall etc.

Margaret's frustration finally snapped whilst doing a national curriculum test. She couldn't do it, but could have no help and she had an outburst in which she threw the textbook, chair and desk at the headmaster who was taking the class.

Margaret moved up a year and her new teacher was worse with 'the attitude' than the last. Margaret was sat on the 'thick' table. Made to learn 20 spellings a week that she couldn't read, had work torn out of her book because it wasn't right. She developed headaches, psoriasis and had to be taken to school crying, kicking and shouting. Things got so bad I considered taking her out of school.

We were now 18 months since Margaret's initial diagnosis – no help – no assessment. I was battling the education dept trying to cushion Margaret, battling the school and coping with my own frustrations. . . I felt that I was trying to take on the world singlehanded and that everyone was against me. I would feel so confused and isolated I would cry often. My daughter was suffering and I, her mum, felt powerless to help her, I felt so useless.

. . . Margaret has started senior school this term. The school have been very responsive to Margaret's needs so far. . .

The biggest stress factors for me were the reaction of others, the isolation and the feeling of being a small useless fish, battling alone, the visible mental and emotional turmoil being suffered by my daughter, and the guilt felt at not being able to achieve anything positive for her . . .

People are ignorant to the facts, will not acknowledge dyslexia and will not help these children. Parents are left to battle alone and put the pieces back in their child's life. A battle for the future of all 'Margarets' has begun and must be kept up until children of the future can have their educational and emotional needs met – as all children should.

I hope I have been able to give some insight into the problem. It is very difficult to explain the feelings. I hope you achieve publishing something, every little that brings the issues of dyslexia to light are in my eyes most welcome, it is the only way to achieving recognition of a common problem that causes so much heartache to so many children and their parents.

Yours sincerely
Mrs Karen Dodd

Chapter 2
Case studies and some recent research

ANGELA J. FAWCETT

In this chapter, I shall present the stories of some of the children and adults I have worked with over the last decade or so, starting with the history of my own son Matthew in his struggle to achieve his potential. Then I shall consider the underlying causes of the stress dyslexic children suffer, in particular the stress that can be engendered by misperceptions of the level of application of the dyslexic child. I shall illustrate this with some case studies. In the second half of the chapter, by contrast, I shall discuss some of our own research, which for the first time reveals the extraordinary efforts needed for dyslexic children to achieve in a wide range of the most basic skills, even those unrelated to reading. Finally, I shall relate this research back to Matthew, to show how a clearer understanding can alleviate stress for all concerned.

For further information on stress and dyslexia, I refer the interested reader to Rourke and Feurst (1991) and to the *Psychiatric Annals* (1991) special edition on learning disabilities. More recent reviews of socioemotional functioning include Little (1993), whereas research on depression and emotional difficulties has been presented by Wright-Strawderman and Watson (1992), and by Lamm and Epstein (1992).

Stress and dyslexia – a family history

From a personal viewpoint, it is particularly apt that I should be asked to contribute a chapter to this book on stress and dyslexia, because my first involvement with the media was in a television programme about stress in early childhood, in the Baby and Co series chaired by Miriam Stoppard. In the early 1980s, before the proliferation of child abuse which no doubt would now dominate a programme of this type, the emphasis was on issues such as additives and congenital disease, including in this case dyslexia. The producer's brief was to find a child whose problems had been identified in the first year of school, as a result of a stress reaction. This led them to my son Matthew.

My original interest in dyslexia was stimulated by the difficulties experienced by Matthew, who was first diagnosed as dyslexic at the unusually early age of five and a half. As a small child, Matthew was clearly bright and enquiring, with a challenging mind, great confidence in himself and tremendous enthusiasm for life. When he started school, he became withdrawn and introverted, to the extent that his first teacher questioned whether or not he could speak. In spite of his assurances that life had never been so good, it soon became clear that something was badly wrong. This culminated in many broken nights, where Matthew woke crying with pains in his legs, coupled with poor reports of his progress at school. Following his referral to the children's hospital with suspected rheumatoid arthritis, Matthew was referred to the clinical psychologist for investigation of his cross-laterality. In Matthew's case, the discrepancy between his intelligence in the top 1 per cent and his inability at this stage to recognise a single letter was particularly striking. At this stage he had been at school for around 9 months, in a fairly formal environment, where the children were expected to be able to write their name on arrival. Matthew could not even hold the pen, and was still undecided whether to use his right or his left hand! The infant school had tried to give Matthew some help, but this involved completing three-piece jigsaws with the headmistress, with another child whose development had been severely retarded by treatment for leukaemia.

The diagnosis of dyslexia transformed Matthew's life, and his relief was palpable. He explained that he had been particularly concerned by the flash cards that the teacher held up, which other children read with ease. He had assumed, therefore, that he must be stupid. After a weekend with us trying to learn 'Come' (one of the most frequently recurring words in the Ladybird first reader), Matthew could tell us that it was a four-letter word, that it came at the beginning of a sentence, and it must therefore be either come or here, but he still could not read it! The sequence of letters seemed to be useless to him in his attempts to identify the word. The unexpected communication failure between Matthew and his teacher meant that he lost any opportunity to convince her of his intelligence, by revealing the depth of the discrepancy between his spoken and written language. In response to the stress of the school environment, where he was continually asked to perform tasks that he found impossible, Matthew had produced a characteristic response. This response, based on the need to hide his difficulties and appear the same as the other children, in its turn increased his feelings of anxiety and fear of failure. After diagnosis, for the first time for many months, he regained his talkativeness and would approach strangers on the bus, as before, but now to confide that he was dyslexic, and this simply meant that he had to try harder to reach the same level as the other children.

I had foolishly assumed that a diagnosis of dyslexia would in many ways alleviate the stress in itself. Certainly, Matthew had become aware that there was a reason for his difficulties, and no longer saw himself as stupid. However, as any parent can tell you, the identification of the problem is just the beginning of a long slow battle for recognition. The first stage for the family is coming to terms with the problem and the acceptance that there really is a difficulty. Too much time and effort can be wasted in simply denying the situation, which in itself hampers the development of the dyslexic child.

In my search for an explanation for Matthew's difficulties, I had considered (and dismissed) the possibility of dyslexia, because initially I found it difficult to equate what I read of dyslexia as a language-based deficit with my own verbally able child. Rather than showing language difficulties, Matthew was fascinated to the point of obsession with the subtle nuances of meaning in the English language. Nevertheless, if you examined his language more carefully, it was obvious that he experienced some early difficulties in the pronunciation of polysyllabic words, coupled with some confusion over their application. To illustrate this, as a small boy of around five, he had some difficulty in pronouncing elbow and shoulder, producing 'oboe' and 'soldier' as his best attempts. Not only that, he continually mislabelled the two, which led to some confusion when he fell over and hurt himself. Problems such as these suggested an underlying deficit to his apparent competence.

Matthew was reassessed as dyslexic at 7 years of age. In terms of literacy skills, by this stage, when prompted with the letter 's' at the beginning of a word such as 'says', he still failed to recognise the letter 's' at the end. His written performance was even worse, so that his teachers described him as the brightest boy in the class, but able to write less than the little Chinese boy who could not speak English. At this time, a placement in special school was considered, but the local junior school decided that they were prepared to take Matthew, in spite of his difficulties. It was an uphill struggle to ensure that Matthew reached the appropriate reading level for his age, but we were fortunate enough to receive help from a friend, a junior schoolteacher with a belief in the merits of a structured approach. He taught Matthew on a voluntary basis for 2 hours each week, from his sixth birthday, until he reached secondary school, and in the process developed a lifelong interest in the anomaly of dyslexia. The work he set involved Matthew laboriously completing several exercises at home each week, always pitched at his level of understanding to maintain his interest in the task. As a young child, there were times when Matthew resented the level of commitment involved in this work, when other children his age were playing. The turning point came after about 6 months of instruction, when we took the gamble of allowing Matthew to decide for himself whether to continue with the lessons or not. Fortunately, he opted to continue.

Nevertheless, Matthew's slowness in producing the work he was set and his difficulty in following instructions at junior school nearly undid all the good work that had been achieved. Following a difficult term with his first teacher at junior school, who was naturally enough irritated by Matthew's vagaries, he developed a stammer. During this year, the educational psychologist came into school to attempt to resolve a situation that was becoming increasingly stressful for Matthew. His teacher believed that he simply refused to complete his work. In a one-to-one situation, in an empty classroom at break, he achieved much more and therefore it was assumed that he could maintain this level, if he wished, in the normal classroom situation. By the end of that year, his teacher admitted that she had misunderstood Matthew's problems and had assumed that he was being difficult when he failed to follow instructions. By this stage, she had realised that Matthew was a cooperative boy, with a wide knowledge base, who could produce the correct answer orally. However, she no longer felt able to question him, because his stammer embarrassed the rest of the class.

At this stage, Matthew first encountered the sponsored spell and the written examination. The children were asked to learn 150 words, appropriate for children aged 7–11, and to collect sponsors. Matthew became sick with worry at the prospect of this test. I therefore contacted the school to check whether participation was compulsory. The head was very reassuring, and said that no one need collect sponsors, but of course they must all attempt the test. For the first time, I took the decision to keep Matthew away from school for the test, but we sent the sponsorship money to add to the school funds. This seems to me to be a useful illustration of the way that the education system can fail to understand the problems of dyslexic children. Following this sponsored spell, Matthew found it difficult to cope with the weekly 20 spellings, and the educational psychologist negotiated with the school to allow him to opt out for a few weeks. The responsibility was left with Matthew to opt in again when he felt able to cope. Within 3 weeks, much to our pride, he had started again, but with 10 simpler spellings, so that he had some hope of achieving them. This was by contrast with the spellings he had struggled with, the list of topic words, which at Easter included Mary Magdalene, Judas Iscariot and Gethsemane, and at other times included champagne and shampoo in the same list. Interestingly enough, my husband tried out the Easter list on his colleagues at work, and only one adult out of 20 in an office environment gained full marks. We adopted a similar strategy of shielding Matthew from the first formal examinations, when he was just eight, which were taken in the hall under examination conditions. For many weeks before the examinations, his teacher had warned him that he would get nothing in them. On this occasion, Matthew had become very anxious, and complained of sickness and sore throat. This time I checked with our local doctor, who found the whole system of testing such young children barbaric and recommended that I keep Matthew at home. These were the only times when we allowed Matthew to stay away from school, to avoid humiliation which we felt would be counterproductive.

Matthew's problems were compounded in the second year of junior school by his experience of a very pleasant but overzealous teacher, who sent home nine pieces of homework some nights, in her efforts to ensure that Matthew had completed as much work as the rest of the class. Matthew became anxious and started trying to get up very early in the morning to complete the work. At this stage, we decided that it might be appropriate to change schools and send Matthew to a school that was a little less formal. However, the situation was defused by intervention from the head, who dictated the work to Matthew and wrote down his response, thus completing the allocated work in 30 minutes. There then followed two of Matthew's happier school years, with teachers who understood and liked him. By the time he reached secondary school, his reading was adequate but slow, but he needed a further year in the Special Needs class to improve his writing and spelling skills.

Living in close proximity to the problem, I was inevitably faced with constant exposure to a whole series of dyslexic vagaries, such as confusion over times, days and even the general organisation of life. The pervasiveness of the deficit, in fact, again led me to question whether the problems we were dealing with could be dyslexic in origin. Most striking of all, in retrospect, was the clumsiness which led to a constant series of accidents ranging in severity from the regularly spilt drinks to a suspected broken back! But at the time, it was the simplest manifestations of dyslexia that appeared the most puzzling, in particular the problems with even the simplest rote learnt material. To illustrate this, at junior school, Matthew constantly muddled breakfast and supper (because you eat cereal at both), and he only grasped the difference when explicitly taught that breakfast was the first meal in the day, because it is then that you break your fast. He continues to make this mistake occasionally to this day, and he has never grasped the difference between lunch and tea-time.

At secondary school, he continued to exasperate his teachers with his forgetfulness, until they realised that this was just one manifestation of a more generalised memory problem. The school operated a fortnightly timetable. Matthew, however, could never work out whether it was week 1 or week 2, and anyway he had lost his timetable. At this stage, of course, pupils no longer have desks, and need to bring the appropriate books daily. Matthew's response was to fill his large bag to overflowing with every book he possessed, and then delve fruitlessly in its depths for the appropriate books. Moreover, he would spend many hours completing his homework, only to leave it crumpled in the bottom of his bag, because he could not find the pigeon holes to hand the work in. A memorable instance was the occasion when, having been sent home for a forgotten book, he simply forgot that he had put some sausages under the grill and set fire to the house. Strangely enough, Matthew's response to this near disaster endeared him to his teachers, and from that stage forward he had reached a turning point. The Special Needs teacher, a woman with a very clear understanding of dyslexia, set up a support system for Matthew, which for the first time allowed him to do himself justice. He simply reported to her each morning, and she checked that he had handed in his homework. At the end of the day, she checked that he had copied down his homework correctly. This recognition that his efforts to achieve were hampered by his memory difficulties transformed the situation for Matthew. Just how much progress we had made became evident during his GCSEs, when one of the more resistant members of staff exclaimed 'That boy has difficulties – he does tremendously well!', in response to my query about the regularity of presentation of his homework. This is not to say that everything became perfect, and Matthew now admits to the odd day where he pretended to be sick, presenting me with a mixture of orange juice and flour, to justify his claims. It seems to me that it is simply not possible for even the most motivated child constantly to maintain the degree of effort and concentration necessary to become a successful dyslexic.

The need to research dyslexia

Consequently, it soon became evident that, at least in Matthew's case, the dyslexic deficit was expressed in a whole range of areas more generalised than the traditionally accepted reading, spelling and language. At the same time I was well aware that the most difficult part of coping with any handicap lies in accepting and coming to terms with a range of possible outcomes. Therefore, I set out to research the condition systematically, in as wide a range of dyslexic children of similar age as I could find. Eventually, I found myself armed with a battery of anecdotal evidence of generalised deficits in other dyslexic children – for instance, of clumsiness and difficulty in rote learning – gleaned from my dialogues with parents, teachers and children. It seemed that I was not alone in noting these bizarre manifestations of the problem, and clinicians in the field had a range of similar observations to report. On the other hand, it was clear that perceptions of dyslexia, unfortunately, remained very much dependent on the viewpoint of the observer. This is illustrated by a series of vignettes on the dyslexic child, drawn from interviews with parents and teachers and from school reports.

The teachers

Unsympathetic head (of 7 year old)

He's not dyslexic – he's just a silly little boy who won't concentrate for more than 10 seconds: what he needs is a good kick up the backside!

Exasperated (but supportive) teacher (of 14 year old)

This year Mark has put in the very minimum of effort. He arrives at lessons ill-prepared, his homework is rarely, if ever, handed in and his work is scrappily presented. He is his own worst enemy!

The parents

Baffled parent

Alan just keeps losing things – he put his coat in the locker so it wouldn't get lost, but then he lost the key, and now he can't even remember which locker it was – he'd lose his own head if it wasn't joined on!

Depressed parent

The depressing thing is that although we've gone over the word 20 times this weekend, he still doesn't seem to be any better at spelling it!

Desperate parent

He's been in the remedial reading group for 5 years now, but I'm sure he's reading worse now than when he was 8 years old.

My need to understand the enigma of dyslexia led me to return to study as a mature student, and altered the whole course of my life. An attempt to impose some meaning and order on such apparently disparate phenomena as these led me to the formulation of my research hypotheses. The theoretical implications of this research will be discussed later in this chapter. Matthew, by the age of 14, would no longer be diagnosed as dyslexic in terms of his reading, but interestingly enough continued to show all the associated difficulties in spelling, clumsiness, memory and organisation which characterise the dyslexic.

I shall return to Matthew later in this chapter, when I discuss the continued stress attributable to dyslexia in adolescence. First, however, I shall discuss some of the major issues in diagnosing a child as dyslexic.

To label or not to label?

Readers of this book will all be familiar with the reluctance in educational circles to label children as dyslexic, in case the child shelters behind this diagnosis and uses it as an excuse for failure. Having read my own family history, it should come as no surprise to the reader that I do not subscribe to this view. It is important in such cases to consider the alternative labels that may be wrongly applied to the child: these range from stupid, not very bright, a late developer, over-anxious or emotionally disturbed, to lazy and lacks concentration, or even in the worst case scenario, aggressive, uncooperative and difficult. These labels offer no solutions. A diagnosis of dyslexia, by contrast, provides not only a description of the range of symptoms but also a prescription for how to help the child to overcome his or her difficulties.

Readers may also be familiar with the well-worn concept of 'reading readiness' and 'late developers'. This school of thought suggests that, as with potty training, it is better to wait until the child is ready, and then they will simply make up the lost ground in their own good time. The problem is that reading is not a bit like potty training, mainly because it is not an all-or-none experience. Reading is based on the interplay of a large range of subskills, all of which must be in place before progress can be made to the next stage. The child who fails to achieve fluency in tasks such as letter naming falls further and further behind, until it becomes impossible to make up the backlog. Unfortunately, the corrosive effects of this failure can damage the psyche irretrievably, producing the 'Matthew effect' (Stanovich, 1986) ('Unto every one that hath shall be given, and he shall have abundance; but from him that hath not shall be taken away even that which he hath' – *Matthew*, xxv, 29). This culminates in both depressed achievement and depressed self-concept. The longer the problem goes unrecognised, the greater the potential effects. Research suggests a steady deterioration in the prognosis for reading, directly related to the number of years before dyslexia is diagnosed (Strag, 1972). On the other hand, most children whose dyslexia is identified at around the age of 6–7 years reach the appropriate reading level by the time they reach secondary school.

Sources of stress

It is hardly surprising that life is stressful for a dyslexic child who is failing within the school system. One might assume, however, that the situation for successful dyslexic children, with no overt reading difficulties and minimal spelling problems, might well be very different. Quite the contrary. My experience and interactions with a range of dyslexic adults, including my own husband, strongly suggest that this is not so. Although the plight of the low-achieving dyslexic is more severe, life for any dyslexic remains fraught with difficulties. Is this simply because they are still carrying the burden of their earlier struggles? The most plausible explanation is that there can be more than one source of stress. For underachieving dyslexics, there are external pressures from school and home to reach an acceptable level of literacy. However, there is an added source of stress for dyslexics, whatever their level of achievement, namely the sheer amount of effort needed just to keep pace with life. A useful analogy here might be that of the dyslexic constantly running on a treadmill, just to stay in one place in a range of skills that others acquire with ease.

The remainder of this chapter is divided into two parts. First, I address the role of external pressures from the school and home as a contributory factor in the stress that dyslexics suffer, illustrating this with some case studies. Then I shall go on to describe some of my own research, which for the first time attempts to quantify internal sources of stress in dyslexia, in particular the amount of effort required just to achieve normal performance. This research explains the fragility of the skills acquired in dyslexia, the problems in concentration identified in dyslexia, and the good and bad days which have been so widely documented. However, first, let us consider external sources of stress.

It is tempting to assume that the education system must take the major responsibility for the stress that is suffered by children with dyslexia. Certainly, as I shall go on to show, lack of understanding of the problem within the teaching profession means that children with dyslexia suffer more than they need. This failure to understand dyslexia is not the fault of the teacher, but can be attributed to failure to train teachers adequately in the recognition of dyslexia. A standard response to the dyslexic child is one of exasperation – why should a child who appears to be verbally able show such inordinate difficulty in grasping skills that other children acquire with relative ease? I think that we have all been guilty at some stage of responses of this type. Possibly more deleterious for the child is an underestimation of the child's abilities, coupled with access to a restricted curriculum within the Special Needs class. Of course many teachers are particularly skilled in detecting the type of anomalous performance that characterises dyslexia. Others, in spite of training in the warning signs, tend to underestimate the incidence of dyslexia and are unprepared to work with the problem if they ever come across it. However, unlike many of the other developmental disorders (such as autism), dyslexia is relatively common, with around 5% incidence regularly identified in Western countries (e.g. Badian, 1984; Jorm et al., 1986). This means that every classroom will contain at least one dyslexic child. When teachers have heard a lecture on dyslexia it is not unusual to witness their reassessment of the pupils with whom they have worked in the past, coupled with a belated realisation that these children were classically dyslexic.

An interesting reflection of teachers' perceptions may be the fact that, particularly in America, attention deficit–hyperactivity disorder (ADHD) is also commonly diagnosed in conjunction with dyslexia. The basis for this diagnosis is typically the Connor's Behavioural Questionnaire, derived from teachers' impressions of the application children show within the school (Holborrow and Berry, 1986). Indeed, many positive indicators of attention deficit are based on factors such as inability to complete work within an allotted time period, and therefore it is hardly surprising that dyslexic children tend to show a more consistent deficit than other children. The Dunedin epidemiological study, for example

(McGee and Share, 1988), found that about 80% of 11 year olds identified as ADHD had dyslexia, which led the authors to argue that for these children their attentional deficits were really secondary to their learning disabilities. Even in this country, the concept of the dyslexic child with poor concentration and short attention span has become something of a stereotype.

By contrast with this interpretation, our own research (Nicolson and Fawcett, 1990), which I describe in greater detail later in this chapter, shows that children with dyslexia actually input considerably greater resources in all skills, not just literacy skills, to achieve the same level of performance as other children. In basic or primitive skills, which form the building blocks for more complex skills, they even show deficits in comparison with younger reading age controls (Nicolson and Fawcett, 1993). In spite of all their efforts, they are often less successful in literacy skills, which demand the smooth interplay of a range of basic skills. Misinterpretation of these efforts as laziness or lack of attention increases the frustration of the dyslexic child, and could well provoke confrontational behaviour in one personality type or depression in another.

This brings us to the second potential source of stress: the parents. Although many enlightened parents would defend their offspring at all costs, there are others with less knowledge of education who take on board the negative perceptions of the school, and endorse them. The situation for a child who is misunderstood at school and at home is particularly stressful. For many parents, the difficulties their child suffers are an unpleasant reminder of their own experiences in school. The feelings of ineptitude and frustration that they suffered at that time, when the education system was less sympathetic to dyslexia, may render them impotent to deal with their current situation. My own husband, for example, has painful memories of one teacher's instructions to 'Stand in the bin – you're rubbish!'. The smell of cooking, new paint and disinfectant that permeates most schools can still bring back his feelings of sickness and fear.

However, it is also worth emphasising here that the child's own perceptions may play a role in his or her difficulties. It may not be simply the failure to learn within the school environment that places such stress on the child with dyslexia. There is a body of evidence now accruing which suggests that differences in the brain organisation of dyslexic children may predispose them to problems with organisational and social skills (see, for example, Rourke and Feurst, 1991; see also Badian, 1992). In terms of emotional stability, the literature suggests a threefold increase in psychiatric diagnoses in children with dyslexia (Duane, 1991), in particular of conduct disorder and depression. Of course, it is difficult to establish whether this is a cause, an effect or simply correlated with dyslexia. However, it might be argued that these problems are natural sequelae of the years of failure, or the need constantly to strive to achieve even average marks within the school system.

Finally, an additive factor in the stress engendered by dyslexia is the guilt that all those involved in this situation may suffer. The teacher may blame her- or himself for failure to achieve any worthwhile improvement in the skills of a child who is clearly bright. The parents experience guilt because they have inadvertently passed their difficulties on to their child, and they themselves do not have the necessary skills to help him or her. Sensing these undercurrents, the child may blame him- or herself for letting down both parents and teachers. This guilt can easily turn to anger and blame for each other, rendering the situation untenable and potentially explosive.

In the case studies that follow, you will note that there is an imbalance between males and females – this is because typically four times as many boys as girls are diagnosed as dyslexic. I shall attempt to show that, in terms of stress, dyslexia has repercussions throughout life, and for dyslexics at all levels of achievement. Let me illustrate this for you.

The preschool child

There is evidence for a strong hereditary component in dyslexia. In fact, there is between a 14 and 17 per cent chance of being dyslexic if your mother or father is dyslexic (Pennington, 1991). The child I describe here, Adam, is the second child in a family of three. The father (a dyslexic student, to whom I will return later in these case studies) and the eldest daughter are also dyslexic. Adam was typical of a certain type of dyslexic child, slow to develop language and with speech problems in articulation which were identified preschool and resistant to speech and language therapy. He presents as a pleasant but confused small boy, very willing to learn, but with difficulties in almost every aspect of language and literacy. His failure to benefit from speech and language therapy led to a referral to our department for testing. In spite of the fact that his problems were clear to most professionals who came in contact with him, his teacher was not unduly concerned by his progress, and it was decided that the parents were being overanxious. It was also necessary to wait for Adam to fall 2 years behind in his reading before dyslexia could be diagnosed. In the interim, since the breakdown of his parent's marriage, the decision has been taken to conceal the family history of dyslexia from the new school. Given that there are now presumably emotional difficulties consequent on the split, it is not clear how this child will progress, and his lack of skill in language may well be interpreted as indicative of low potential.

The junior school child

Jacob

Jacob's difficulties were originally diagnosed at the Dyslexia Institute, when he was aged 8;6 years, and around 2 years behind in his reading and 3 years in his spelling. There was a marked family history of dyslexia: his grandfather had left school unable to read and write, his mother had experienced difficulties and all six of his cousins had been diagnosed as dyslexic. His family had experienced considerable difficulty in obtaining any recognition of Jacob's difficulties from his school, because the area in which he lived was fairly mixed in terms of socioeconomic intake. It was therefore suggested that his performance was not necessarily the worst in the class. The stress he had endured had resulted in Jacob losing all his hair. He found it particularly galling to be consigned to the remedial class, because he realised that many of the other children were simply not very bright. By secondary school age, he had made intense and successful efforts to overcome his reading difficulties, although his spelling was still dire (see Thomson, 1984, for a comparison of reading and spelling problems). When I re-tested him again at the age of 15, he continued to show problems with speed of processing and short-term memory, to the extent that his scores on the IQ tests had dropped. This was not because Jacob had deteriorated in real terms, simply that he had not made the expected improvement with age. Jacob was not allowed to attempt GCE, because he was not considered to be of the appropriate calibre, in spite of the efforts he and his parents made to obtain recognition of his difficulties. We last worked together when Jacob was around 17, when he developed problems with kidney failure and dropped out of my research panel. He has since made some unsuccessful attempts at further education, and is currently looking for work.

Benjamin

The effects of stress on Benjamin were in many ways similar to those on Jacob. Benjamin and his older brother both had problems in literacy, but their mother, an ex-teacher, had put in considerable effort to help them with their reading. This meant that parental concern over the boys' progress was dismissed, because there were other children in the class with similar or greater problems in reading. Benjamin was more severely affected by the attendant stress than his brother, and lost over a stone in weight. By the age of 7+, Benjamin was unable to write his own name, and begged to change it to Ben. The situation came to a head following a school trip to a Police station, which Benjamin had clearly enjoyed, when his teachers claimed that he simply refused pointblank to write a thank-you letter. By this stage Benjamin had changed from a compliant and delightful boy, to a stubborn and angry child, and the school became confrontational about his refusal to complete his work. Eventually, he burst into tears at home, admitted that he was simply unable to write the letter, that he realised that he wrote like a baby and knew that he was different from the other children. He finally completed the letter by copying his mother's writing, thus resolving the issue for the time being. However, nothing had yet been done about the underlying problem. In the following year, he became more and more withdrawn, lost a stone and a half in weight, and suffered from blinding headaches, attacks of weeping and reluctance to attend school. This led to a referral to the children's hospital, where Benjamin was given an EEG and a brain scan. There was no evidence of any medical problem. The situation was resolved when his parents had both the boys tested for dyslexia at the local Dyslexia Institute and removed them from their local school to place them in a more sympathetic environment. Here Benjamin flourished, regained his lost weight and began to enjoy school. By the age of 11, he was second in science within a highly academic environment, but nevertheless, he still shows a motor coordination problem with his handwriting.

Dominic

Of course, not all children react to stress by becoming withdrawn and introverted, and losing their hair or stones in weight. It is possibly just as common, dependent on the basic personality of the child, to adopt a 'devil may care' response to failure. In many ways it is possible to save face among your peer group by pretending that you do not care whether or not you succeed in the school setting. Taken to extremes, a dyslexic child may develop behavioural problems, as a consequence of a sloppy approach to work as a smoke screen to hide the fact that he cannot cope. This was the case with Dominic, who had reached the age of nine before his problems with literacy were diagnosed. This was undoubtedly because they were masked by even more severe behavioural problems. I first met Dominic when he was withdrawn from school for poor behaviour and came into the Psychology Department. His school complained that Dominic found it impossible to concentrate and disrupted the other children with his antics. Dominic presented to an adult as an appealing boy with an impish sense of humour and prodigious skill in drawing. There was no trace of problems in concentration as he produced a whole family of space monsters for me. However, it was particularly striking that when he wished to name these monsters, he needed an adult to spell even the simplest word. This led me to question whether or not Dominic might be dyslexic, and to raise the issue with his father, a psychologist, who was himself dyslexic. The situation came to a head when Dominic ran away from school, and started to walk the 4 miles to his house. His teacher followed him in the car and returned him to school, where he threw mud in the playground. When his teacher asked him to stop this, Dominic responded by throwing mud at her and was subsequently expelled. In Dominic's case, his school had been unable to identify the real cause of the problem, because he had used bad behaviour as a smoke screen to hide his inability to cope with literacy skills. Even his own father, a skilled and sensitive clinician, could not put his finger on the underlying difficulties, possibly because he was himself dyslexic. A full test of Dominic's abilities showed that he was a boy of superior intelligence with severe difficulties in literacy. Since this diagnosis his behaviour has settled down, although he needed to move to several schools, including one for children with behavioural difficulties, before he found one that was sympathetic to his dyslexia. Dominic is currently successfully studying media at sixth form college.

The adolescent

It is at this stage that I shall return to consider the progress of my own son, Matthew. With considerable support from school and home, Matthew had largely overcome his reading difficulties by the time he reached GCSE level. His spelling remained relatively poor, and the speed of his written work significantly slower than that of other children of similar ability. Nevertheless, with extra time allowances for GCSE, he achieved laudable grades and went on to tackle 'A' levels. Here he chose subjects that place an unacceptable burden of written work on most students, not simply those who are dyslexic. He decided to take English literature, history and sociology, in spite of the fact that he was still considerably slowed down by the effort required in reading and writing. However, because his reading skills were improved, the issue of whether or not extra time should be allowed in his examinations was less clear-cut. The school put him in for extra time, on the grounds that they recognised his dyslexia. A short questionnaire was sent out to all the teachers, who agreed that, although his performance was not always exemplary, he was generally a conscientious student who should be allowed extra time because he was still slow to complete his work, and continued to have considerably more difficulty than others of similar ability. In the event, the educational psychologist who dealt with the case found more evidence of emotional difficulties than dyslexia, based on the stammering. This was in spite of a letter from the clinical psychologist who diagnosed the dyslexia to the effect that Matthew's emotional difficulties were a consequence of his learning difficulties. Consequently, Matthew was denied the extra time to which he should have been entitled as a dyslexic. Not only this, he had completed half his examinations before a decision was reached, and each day faced the uncertainty engendered by this failure to reach a decision. The consequent level of stress was unacceptable at a time that is already stressful enough for a candidate with no disability. A subsequent appeal and reassessment confirmed his original diagnosis of dyslexia, but could not raise his grades in the English examination, which he only half completed. If parents with our level of knowledge and experience in the field of dyslexia were impotent in this situation, how much more difficult must it be for less knowledgeable parents to obtain their rights?

Overall, however, the story has a happy ending, with Matthew achieving grades that allowed him to take up a place at university to study politics and philosophy.

Of course, not all dyslexics are so successful – which brings me to my second case study of stress in adolescence, John.

John

I have worked with John since 1985, when he became one of the first members of my research panel, during his placement at a special school in Sheffield. At 10 years old, John presented as a pleasant outgoing boy, with extensive difficulties in the area of language and literacy. His score of high average on the revised Weschler Intelligence Scale for Children test (WISC-R – Wechsler, 1976) was probably an underestimate, because he was slowed down somewhat by his tendency to verbalise when completing each task. His reading was around three and a half years behind his chronological age, which meant that he had barely started. John had problems in almost every area that has been implicated in dyslexia; he was very short sighted, he stammered, he was extremely nervous and some of his movements were clumsy. John was a boy who did not tolerate fools gladly, and would challenge me as an experimenter to justify the tasks that I asked him to complete. He had a wry sense of humour, and the ability to laugh at his own shortcomings. Following several years of remediation at the Dyslexia Institute, John had made impressive gains in his literacy skills, and had even improved his scores on the intelligence tests. He had always had a good measure of support from his parents, and his school and the individual teachers were all sympathetic. In fact his level of support was exceptional. However, the attendant stress and the amount of effort that he constantly needed to input into his work to try and achieve his potential took its toll.

By the time he reached GCSE level, John suffered a nervous breakdown, and was simply no longer able to maintain the level of effort needed to keep up. From that date onwards, John no longer took part in my research panel, moreover the decision was taken to drop anything that could be a potential source of stress. Recently, John has regained some of his confidence and has successfully completed a youth training scheme in horticulture. Nevertheless, his parents are concerned that he may never obtain work.

Adult students

The problem is, if anything, potentially greater for the dyslexic college student than for 'A' level candidates, although many universities now make special arrangements for dyslexics which are less dependent on evidence of reading difficulty, but recognise the effects of spelling deficits.

The two cases I present here are very different in outcome, although in many ways the students involved were similar in their approach, in the type of difficulties they shared and even in their nursing background. They were both of superior intelligence, with a glaring discrepancy between their verbal and written skills.

Connor

Connor was a mature student in the Department of Psychology, whose problems were identified when his essays were graded unsatisfactory because of his grammatical errors. Following a WAIS test (the Wechsler Adult Intelligence Scale – Wechsler, 1986), I established that Connor's intelligence was in the superior range and that his errors were not ungrammatical, but dyslexic in nature. I confirmed this by asking Connor to read back his work, to check that he appreciated that he should use 'the' rather than 'to' before a noun. Connor showed the typical absent-mindedness and organisational deficits that characterise dyslexia. This may be attributed to the difficulties such students have in working memory, which leaves them less spare resources to deal with the organisation of life. This was illustrated perfectly by Connor's marks in the first year statistics examination. In spite of the fact that statistics was not one of Connor's strengths, even he was dismayed by the low marks he had achieved. On enquiring about this, he learned that only one of the two papers had been submitted and marked. The other paper was subsequently retrieved from his statistics workbook, where it had languished ever since Connor had completed the examination and failed to hand it in. The paper was so poorly presented that it was quite clear that it had not been tampered with in any way, and therefore Connor managed to scrape through when it was eventually marked.

At this stage Connor made a decision which in retrospect he was to regret. He had spent many years fighting down the feelings of inadequacy to which dyslexics typically fall prey. As a result of his experiences in education, Connor was embittered and felt that he had been denied his rights. Moreover, he knew that he had areas of weakness, but he was less confident that he had areas of strength. He was therefore reluctant to disclose his problems and adopted a defensive policy of trying to hide his difficulties. He had never suffered any problems in motivation, and adopted the policy of simply working harder and harder to achieve the grades he needed. This technique had paid off well as a mature student at 'A' level, where he had given up any attempts to lead a normal life to dedicate himself to working in the day and studying at night. However, Connor failed to realise quite how dense the workload would be in his chosen field of law. As a lawyer, he decided that an acknowledgement of his dyslexia might carry a stigma, and therefore he did not seek the allowances to which he was entitled. As a consequence, he failed to complete his papers, obtained a 2.2, which limited his options as a barrister, and went on to fail his articles at the first attempt. Eventually, he admitted that he was dyslexic and obtained the grades he needed on a resit. However, Connor is still suffering from his attempt to deny his dyslexia, and since completing his articles has been unable to obtain employment that uses the law degree he fought so hard to achieve.

Richard

By contrast, Richard, the father of Adam, whom I described earlier, was much more successful. If anything, his problems in literacy were greater than Connor's and consequently in his early career he had actually failed his nursing examinations. At this stage he decided that if he was not good enough to become a nurse then he would become a doctor instead. Rather than denying his difficulties, Richard has used the system wherever possible to enable him to achieve his potential. The stress that he suffered in the remedial class at school had made him angry, and it is this anger that carries him through and underpins his determination to succeed. Achieving his medical degree involved studying for many more hours than others of similar ability, and counterbalancing low marks on essay-based examinations with full marks on multichoice examinations. The major difficulties he now faces are in coping with the potentially confusable names of drugs. He has dealt with this by using his disabled student's allowance to purchase a computerised organiser which interfaces with his computer. The frustration he now faces is seeing his children, in particular Adam, who is the mirror image of Richard as a child, suffer as he suffered in school. Richard is not alone in the anger that his treatment in school has engendered. I shall never forget a potential PhD student, who achieved a first in psychology, whose parents had fought against his placement in a special school for children with moderate learning difficulties. His first instinct was to seek out the teacher who had described him as slow, and confront her with the evidence of his success.

Dyslexic adults

Of course, the problem for adults with dyslexia is by no means confined to students. The difficulties faced in school, where the emphasis is placed on subjects in which the dyslexic is disadvantaged, may be compounded in the workplace. The problem here of course is not simply one of literacy, but the speed and efficiency of processing. It is now recognised that a major component of dyslexia is a weakness in handling rapidly presented information (Tallal and Piercy, 1974; Wolf, 1991; Nicolson and Fawcett, 1994a). It may well be that, given ample time, the dyslexic adult can process accurately, but under conditions that are resource intensive, involving high memory load or integration of material from diverse sources, they are at an extreme disadvantage. This may be evident in mundane tasks, such as trying to integrate the information on television programmes from the newspaper, to decide exactly what to watch at 8 p.m., bearing in mind possible overlaps between programmes and regional variations. For some adults, it may mean that they need to devise mnemonics to help them remember seven- or eight-figure numbers which are beyond their memory capacity. In other cases, however, the consequences can be potentially disastrous. This brings me to the case of Simon, the British Rail signalman.

Simon

Simon was an adult in his 40s, who had worked on the railways all his life, predominantly as a signalman. The difficulties he had experienced in learning to read and spell were no problem to him in managing a hand-operated signal system. In fact, by this stage, on any simple test of single word reading, Simon no longer had problems that would be diagnosed as dyslexic in type. However, problems arose when the railway signal system had become computerised. Instead of taking responsibility for a handful of lines, Simon was suddenly asked to monitor 33 lines, with trains represented on a vast overhead illuminated map. Furthermore, to compound his difficulties in coordinating this mass of information, he was expected to remember eight-figure numbers for the individual trains, well beyond the capacity of most people. In addition he needed to make split-second decisions on which line to route the trains, based on very small initial letters, 'f' for forward, 'n' for normal and 'r' for reverse. Awareness of his own shortcomings and the stress this engendered had reduced Simon to a state of imminent breakdown. Following the King's Cross rail disaster, he suffered daily nightmares that his tardiness or errors could precipitate a similar major crash. When he came to me for counselling, I advised Simon that the tasks he was attempting placed unacceptable demands on his processing capacities. Armed with a diagnosis of dyslexia, he approached his employers and was able to make a sideways move into management, which capitalised on his experience, while avoiding his areas of weakness. This was a most successful resolution of an issue that might well have ended in tragedy.

York St John University
Check-Out Receipt

Customer name: CLARKE, Alan Douglas

Title: Dyslexia and stress
ID: 38025004024710
Due: 13/1/2012,23:59

Total items: 1
05/12/2011 10:50
Checked out: 1
Overdue: 0
Hold requests: 1
Ready for pickup: 1

Tel: 01904 876700

The way forward

The suffering that is endured by dyslexics in the current school system and the attendant psychological scarring is hard to quantify, but it impacts on the motivation, the emotional well-being and possibly the behavioural stability of the dyslexic. In many ways, it seems to me that dyslexics are working constantly at the limits of their endurance. Many of us will be familiar with the situation where, under constant pressure, an excellent memory and the most organised personality suddenly give way, with the effect of switching off a computer. For even the most over-stressed academic, this happens just once or twice a year, when conditions become intolerable. I believe that for dyslexics this must be at least a daily occurrence, if not more. In many ways, of course, this may be related to confidence, in that for most of us a belief in our own ability to cope carries us through. For the dyslexic (or even the mature student), I might suggest from personal experience that this knowledge is less certain and more vulnerable to breakdown under stress.

To break out of this destructive cycle, what is needed now is a better theoretical understanding of dyslexia. This has the potential to defuse the guilt and blame, and allow the child, the parents and the teacher to concentrate on the most important task, improving the skills and thereby the self-concepts of the dyslexic. It must be recognised that dyslexia represents a difference in brain organisation (Galaburda et al., 1989) and that, as such, dyslexia cannot be cured but simply remediated. Consequently, dyslexic children grow into dyslexic adults, whether or not their reading difficulties have been overcome. Reading is just the tip of the iceberg of a constellation of difficulties, which impinge on the performance of the dyslexic throughout life (Miles, 1993). Until recently, Tim Miles was unique in attempting to identify these positive symptoms of dyslexia with his Bangor Dyslexia Test (Miles, 1982). Once it has been generally accepted that dyslexia is a constitutional hereditary condition, based on a difference in brain organisation and processing, it becomes possible for teachers and researchers to look out for early signs of difficulty, and thus break into the cycle of dyslexic failure, before motivational deficits have a chance to set in.

In fact, dyslexic children obligingly enough seem to have something within their range of deficits to interest researchers from every conceivable background. Consequently, theories for the cause of the dyslexic deficit are many and varied, and a good deal of time has been spent in trying to establish which one of these theories was correct. Following early evidence of visual difficulties, one of the major achievements of the last 20 years was the identification of deficits in language skills (Vellutino, 1979), and the refinement of the phonological deficit hypothesis (Miles, 1983; Snowling et al., 1986; Stanovich, 1988), which is arguably the consensus theoretical belief of most dyslexia researchers from a psychological background. More recently, problems with visual skills have been re-established as a potential cause of the dyslexic deficit, specifically the threshold for the detection of flicker (Lovegrove et al., 1990), which has been linked via an interdisciplinary project to neuroanatomical abnormalities in the magnocellular pathway (Livingstone et al., 1991).

From a theoretical viewpoint, a programmatic series of experiments from our own laboratory has gone a long way towards revealing one of the underlying causes of dyslexia. In the process, it has revealed the full extent of the stress dyslexic children and adults suffer in their attempts to produce normal performance, and the strengths of the compensatory strategies which allow them to succeed in so many areas.

Let me begin at the beginning, and take you through the stages of our thinking. In my undergraduate research, building on Tim Miles' work on rote learning (1983), I identified problems in reciting the months in my panel of dyslexic children, in comparison with reading age controls. Knowing that dyslexics are often characterised by their naming difficulties, in the early stages of my postgraduate research, I presented a computerised memory for months task, based on selection of the next in the sequence from a list of months presented in random order. I discussed the dyslexic children's inexplicable difficulties with Rod Nicolson, and we decided that their underlying problem might be one of automatisation failure. This would mean that it was difficult for a dyslexic child to become expert in any skill, and Rod suggested that this might best be tested experimentally using motor skills. This led us to challenge the dominant hypothesis that dyslexia is essentially a language-based problem, and consider instead that it might be a more generalised deficit in the acquisition of skills.

Working from the premise that reading is a learned skill, and that all skills, whether cognitive or motor, are learned in the same way (Anderson, 1982), we first examined automaticity in dyslexic children. In the process of learning, the novice has to concentrate on each individual part of the skill he is trying to acquire. An analogy commonly used in describing the development of automaticity is that of learning to drive a car. At first it is necessary to concentrate on each individual component of the driving process, to the exclusion of all others. The expert driver is able to collapse these subskills into a fluid subroutine, leaving plenty of spare capacity for navigating and anticipating the vagaries of other drivers. We already knew that the children we were working with, by definition, had problems with their literacy skills, and so in our search for a skill that is not typically impaired in dyslexia, we decided to test motor skill and, in particular, the most highly practised skill of all – simply balancing on both feet.

Many parents of children with dyslexia recall that their children were unusual in their early years – slow to walk, slow to talk, rather clumsy, maybe a bit accident-prone. These anecdotal reports were distilled by the late Jean Augur into a set of 21 key points (Augur, 1985). As expected many of her points reflected lack of phonological skill. Equally notable, however, were consistent problems with motor skill. Indeed, motor skill problems accounted for Augur's first five points, together with 'Difficulty carrying out more than one instruction at a time' and 'Excessive tiredness due to amount of concentration and effort required'. Interestingly enough, this is one of the earliest acknowledgements of the amount of effort dyslexic children need to input in all areas of their lives. Living with the problem, like Jean, I had reached similar conclusions, but as a psychologist felt the need to check out and quantify my theories.

At the time that we started the balance tests, there was no compelling evidence of motor skill deficits in dyslexic children after the age of 9–10 (Rudel, 1985; although see Haslum, 1989). However, the problem for an automatisation deficit hypothesis (DAD) is that it is really far too powerful. It would predict that dyslexic children would be unable to walk around or even stand up. We argued that dyslexic children obtained their near normal performance after this age by simply working harder, our conscious compensation (CC) hypothesis. My own familiarity with dyslexia had convinced me that dyslexic children could obtain the same results, but by very different means from their non-dyslexic peers. This had been confirmed for us by an in-depth analysis of the reading skills of members of our dyslexic panel who performed at around their chronological age level on single word reading. Any more sensitive tests of literacy revealed that, in spite of their apparent competence, these children were devoting significantly more resources to the task, were slower in their reading performance and more able to use context, overdependence on which has been noted by other researchers (e.g. Stanovich et al., 1985).

Based on these observations, the task we selected to test the motor skills of the children with dyslexia was a dual task, specifically set up to reveal any subtle deficits in balance. The results were consistent with our conscious compensation hypothesis, showing that, although the dyslexic children could balance quite well when just balancing, they were severely impaired when asked to balance while counting. The control children, by contrast, were not affected by the need to perform the tasks concurrently, and therefore their balance was automatic, whereas the dyslexic children's was not. We went on to replicate these results, producing a design where we used three groups of dyslexic children and three groups of controls, allowing us to measure the effects of age and dyslexia on performance. We used a variety of secondary tasks, finally selecting a blindfold balance task as the easiest to interpret.

In spite of the support that this series of tests gave to our DAD hypothesis, they were not designed to illuminate whereabouts in the automatisation process the deficit arose. At this stage, we therefore started a long-term training study with the older children, to determine how easily they learned a motivating computer game involving navigating round a Pacman maze. From this study, we found that the dyslexic children started off very much worse than the control children, in terms of both speed and number of errors, but learned as fast, although they had difficulty in eliminating their errors. However, it is well known that dyslexic children have problems with left and right, and therefore some of their problems could be explained in these terms. As a control, therefore, we ran a further long-term training study, where the children were matched on their baseline speed of performance on simple reaction times (SRTs) to a flash or a tone, with hand or foot. When we put the two tasks together to create a novel choice reaction task, we found that the dyslexic children were initially significantly more slowed than the controls. In spite of the fact that they then learned the task as well as the control children, they never reached the speed of each individual baseline component, whereas the controls, by contrast, could speed their choice reaction time (CRT) performance after practice up to the level of their SRT performance. Extrapolating from these results shows that if skills take around 100 hours to master, it would take a dyslexic child around 1000 hours (10 times as long) to reach the same level. Note that the longer the time taken for a normal child to learn the skill, the greater the predicted decrement – so that for a skill that takes a normal child 400 hours, it would take a dyslexic child 20 times as long, and so on (Nicolson and Fawcett, 1993). A similar, but more pronounced, pattern was found for error elimination in the Pacman training, with dyslexic children making more errors after 10 000 trials than normal children after 100 trials! These figures are really quite astounding, and have profound implications for teaching children with dyslexia. They suggest that it is essential to help the children as early as possible, before bad habits develop and mistakes are perseverated. The most efficient technique would be to identify the children as soon as they start school, and give explicit training from the very start.

The realisation that the major problem for dyslexic children lay not in learning a task but in the very poor baseline from which they started led us to our next programme of experiments. Here we set out to examine a range of primitive skills, everything that anyone had ever considered might be impaired in dyslexia, plus many more besides. Our reason for choosing primitive skills was that we needed to prevent our dyslexic panel from applying their efficient conscious compensation strategies to boost their skills. Moreover, by this stage, we had decided that even the efficiency of the panel's reaction time performance was achieved by a strategy of vigilance and anticipation, which a closer examination of our data confirmed. And so the skills we examined here included psychometric, phonological and working memory, balance and motor skills, and speed of processing. Our results revealed hitherto unsuspected deficits across the range of skills (full details of which are provided in Fawcett and Nicolson, 1994a,b, 1995). Arguably, our most striking findings over-all were that the 17-year-old dyslexics were rarely achieving any better performance than our 8-year-old controls. It has recently been empha-sised that much more may be learnt from comparison with their reading age than their chronological age controls (Bryant and Goswami, 1986). Here, however, we were finding that our dyslexic 17 year olds were performing at the level of children around half their age. In terms of our driving analogy, learning skills for our dyslexic children were somewhat akin to continually driving through a foreign country. It is possible, but at the expense of constant vigilance and an unacceptable cost in resources.

Naturally enough, these results have caused consternation among the dyslexia community and practitioners working in the field. However, it is worth emphasising here that this evidence for a generalised deficit does not mean dyslexics are simply stupid. Quite the reverse, in fact. We believe that the cognitive system (including intelligence) is functioning at normal or above normal levels, as witnessed by the high achievement levels of many adults with dyslexia (West, 1991). It may well be, in fact, that these children start off with a constant struggle in acquiring literacy, and then simply carry on fighting throughout their adult lives to reach heights to which others cannot aspire

One of the more heated recent debates revolves around the role of intelligence, that is, whether there are any differences between dyslexic children, whose failure is surprising, and slow learners, whose failure is not (e.g. Siegel, 1989). We have recently started to compare the perfor-mance of our dyslexic panels with children with intelligence levels of around 70–85 on the WISC test at diagnosis. Our overall aims here were twofold: first, to establish whether or not the phonological deficits iden-tified in dyslexia were found in children of low ability; and second to attempt to produce a series of diagnostic tests that were capable of differentiating between dyslexics and slow learners. Interestingly enough, the slow-learning children had difficulties in most of the primi-tive skills that we tested, although their balance performance was not necessarily as impaired as that of the dyslexic children by the addition of a blindfold. Similarly, they showed a different profile on the SRTs, show-ing little effect of the addition of a choice reaction on their poor baseline SRT. The pattern of results obtained, however, was not yet distinctive enough to discriminate the two groups reliably, but they pointed the way to further research.

Existing theories for the cause of dyslexia were not able to handle all the results from our primitive skills battery, although all these theories contribute substantially to our understanding of dyslexia. Moreover, even our own automatisation deficit hypothesis, although a useful characterisation of the pattern of deficits shown, is mainly descriptive. At this stage, we sought to link our own theories back to the underlying neurophysiology. Consideration of the pattern of deficits that we had identified led us to consider the potential role of the cerebellum in dyslexia. Until recently, the cerebellum has been largely dismissed, in spite of the fact that it is well known that it is involved in motor skill. The fact that the cerebellum has evolved to an unprecedented size in humans compared with other primates was largely explained in terms of bipedal walking. A series of experiments have now suggested that the cerebellum is critically involved in learning, not just in motor skills, but also in any task that demands 'language dexterity' (Leiner et al., 1989), which seemed to us to be an excellent description of the deficit in dyslexic performance. This involvement of the cerebellum in language was found even when only memory is involved, without any overt articulation to introduce motor skills (Paulesu et al., 1993). Working on this premise, we presented a series of tasks to our dyslexic panels, performances on which have been found to characterise cerebellar patients (Ivry and Keele, 1989). To our excitement, we identified a similar dissociation in dyslexia to that identified in the cerebellar patients, namely a deficit in time estimation but not an equivalent control task, loudness estimation. In work funded by the Medical Research Council, we set out to investigate basic cerebellar skills, assuming that there would be subtle manifestations of deficit which must be unmasked by dual task manipulations of task complexity. Somewhat to our surprise, we unearthed problems in a range of basic cerebellar tests drawn from a post-war medical book, based on the deficits found in patients with wounds to their cerebellum (Dow and Moruzzi, 1958).

Finally, we set out to quantify the relative size of the deficits in all the primitive and cerebellar skills in our panel (using standard scores to compare the performance of each child with the mean and standard deviation of their control group) to establish which of the existing theories was best supported by the data. We found, as we had always suspected, that actually we were all right! There were problems in phonological skills, memory, speed, balance and cerebellar tasks. However, the strongest and most consistent deficits were in phonological skills and balance, particularly the simpler cerebellar tests. These included simply pushing a blindfold child in the back with one finger and noting the response, a task that is particularly straightforward both to administer and to score. The size of the cerebellar deficits and the incidence among our dyslexic panel were among the highest in our battery of tests, equivalent to the spelling deficits, which typically were more severe than the reading deficits. Interestingly enough, we found a similar pattern of results in the boys at Mark College, a school for dyslexic boys in Somerset, having mounted an expedition to test around half of their 80 students. However, these boys have made considerable strides in their phonological skills, confirming that the phonological deficits are amenable to good remediation techniques.

Based on these findings, we have now reached the stage where we have put together a screening test for positive signs of dyslexia, which may be applied in the first term of school. The DEST test (Nicolson and Fawcett, 1994b) is based on positive indicators of balance, speed and cerebellar deficits, coupled with the well-known phonological deficit. The exciting thing about our test is that it taps natural skills, rather than taught skills, is independent of home and school training effects, and above all is non-threatening. As a lifespan test, it can therefore be applied not only to children before they fail to learn to read, but also to adults who are relatively skilled in literacy. The results of a recent survey (Nicolson et al., 1993) suggest that this will be welcomed by the dyslexia community. This is confirmed by the interest our early screening test has engendered, with over 1000 enquiries from parents and teachers. We are currently evaluating our test in selected schools nationwide, and it is hoped that the Psychological Corporation will develop the test.

Finally, let us consider what the outcome might be in terms of stress reduction if children at risk for dyslexia could be identified via whole school screening in reception, and support provided to prevent their failure. Matthew is an interesting case in point, because, of course, his problems were identified exceptionally early. Nevertheless, he contin- ued to suffer stress, which at times became insupportable. However, at this stage understanding of dyslexia in young children was not suffi- ciently advanced to ensure appropriate provision in school. Many of his early difficulties could be attributed to his attempts to hide his dyslexia, because he mistakenly feared that he might be stupid. From that stage on, he was given the help he needed to progress, but not necessarily the understanding. Although we encountered excellent teachers who gave Matthew every support, in spite of their lack of knowledge of the condi- tion, we also encountered teachers who misunderstood. In spite of the recognition of his difficulties, at every open night some teacher would express surprise that Matthew was dyslexic. For a child like Matthew, who manages to overcome reading problems, the ability to interact well with teachers is critical. It is essential to enlist their aid and their sympa- thy for the condition, rather than arouse their irritation by apparently slap-dash work. Similarly, it is crucial that the parents adopt the right mix of support and encouragement, and maintain their equanimity, in spite of the scepticism that they may encounter within the education system. How much easier it would all be if the knowledge of how to handle dyslexia equalled that of sensory deficits in the early school years. It is not so many years since children with visual or auditory deficits were condemned to years of failure before their condition was recognised. Hopefully, before the turn of the century identification of dyslexia will be as standard as the eye test all children are routinely given at school entry.

For the first time, we could be on the brink of sidestepping the cycle of motivational deficits that permeates the current system. In terms of the stress suffered by dyslexic children and their families at all ages, we have the chance to transform the future. Although life for dyslexics may always entail an element of struggle, we can ensure that they are able to express their potential freed from the debilitating consequences of their literacy difficulties.

References

Anderson JR (1982). Acquisition of cognitive skill. *Psychological Review* **89**: 369–406.

Augur J (1985). Guidelines for teachers, parents and learners. In M Snowling (Ed.), *Children's Written Language Difficulties*. Windsor: NFER-Nelson.

Badian NA (1984). Reading disability in an epidemiological context: Incidence and environmental correlates. *Journal of Learning Disabilities* **17**: 129–36.

Badian NA (1992). Nonverbal learning disability, school behaviour and dyslexia. *Annals of Dyslexia* **42**: 159–79.

Bryant P, Goswami U (1986). Strengths and weaknesses of the reading level design. *Psychological Bulletin* **100**: 101–3.

Dow RS, Moruzzi G (1958). *The Physiology and Pathology of the Cerebellum*. Minneapolis: University of Minnesota Press.

Duane DD (1991). Dyslexia: neurobiological and behavioural correlates. *Psychiatric Annals* **21**: 703–8.

Fawcett AJ, Nicolson RI (1994a). Persistent deficits in motor skill for children with dyslexia. *Journal of Motor Behaviour* in press.

Fawcett AJ, Nicolson RI (1994b). Naming speed in children with dyslexia. *Journal of Learning Disabilities* **27**: 641–7.

Fawcett AJ, Nicolson RI (1995). Persistence of phonological awareness deficits in older children with dyslexia. *Reading and Writing* in press.

Galaburda AM, Rosen GD, Sherman GF (1989). The neural origin of developmental dyslexia: Implications for medicine, neurology and cognition. In AM Galaburda (Ed.), *From Reading to Neurons*. Cambridge, MA: MIT Press.

Haslum MN (1989). Predictors of dyslexia? *Irish Journal of Psychology* **10**: 622–30.

Holborrow PL, Berry PS (1986). Hyperactivity and learning difficulties. *Journal of Learning Disabilities* **19**: 426–31.

Ivry RB, Keele SW (1989). Timing functions of the cerebellum. *Journal of Cognitive Neuroscience* **1**: 136–52.

Jorm AF, Share DL, McLean R, Matthews D (1986). Cognitive factors at school entry predictive of specific reading retardation and general reading backwardness: A research note. *Journal of Child Psychology and Psychiatry and Allied Disciplines* **27**: 45–54.

Lamm O, Epstein R (1992). Specific reading impairments – are they to be associated with emotional difficulties? *Journal of Learning Disabilities* **25**: 605–15.

Leiner HC, Leiner AL, Dow RS (1989) Reappraising the cerebellum: what does the hindbrain contribute to the forebrain? *Behavioural Neuroscience* **103**: 998–1008.

Little SS (1993). Nonverbal learning difficulties and socioemotional functioning: A review of recent literature. *Journal of Learning Disabilities* **26**: 653–65.

Livingstone MS, Rosen GD, Drislane FW, Galaburda AM (1991). Physiological and anatomical evidence for a magnocellular deficit in developmental dyslexia. *Proceedings of the National Academy of Sciences of the USA* **88**: 7943–7.

Lovegrove WJ, Garzia RP, Nicholson SB (1990). Experimental evidence of a transient system deficit in specific reading disability. *Journal of the American Optometric Association* 61: 137–46.

McGee R, Share DL (1988). Attention deficit disorder–hyperactivity and academic failure: Which comes first and what should be treated? *Journal of the American Academy of Child and Adolescent Psychiatry* 27: 318–25.

Miles TR (1982). *The Bangor Dyslexia Test*. Cambridgeshire: LDA.

Miles TR (1983). *Dyslexia: the Pattern of Difficulties*. London: Granada.

Miles TR (1993). *Dyslexia: the Pattern of Difficulties*, 2nd edn. London: Whurr.

Nicolson RI, Fawcett AJ (1990). Automaticity: a new framework for dyslexia research? *Cognition* 30: 159–82.

Nicolson RI, Fawcett AJ (1993). Children with dyslexia acquire skill more slowly. *Proceedings of the 15th Conference of the Cognitive Science Society*, University of Colorado, Boulder.

Nicolson RI, Fawcett AJ (1994a). Reaction times and dyslexia. *Quarterly Journal of Experimental Psychology* 47A: 29–48.

Nicolson RI, Fawcett AJ (1994b). *The DEST Screening Test*. Sidcup: The Psychological Corporation.

Nicolson RI, Fawcett AJ (1994c). Early identification: New research. Paper presented to the Dyslexia Institute Guild, Innovations in SpLD/Dyslexia, December 1994.

Nicolson RI, Fawcett AJ, Miles TR (1993). Feasibility study for the development of a computerised screening text for dyslexia in adults. *Employment Department, Report OL176*. Employment Department, Sheffield.

Paulesu E, Frith CD, Frackowiak RJ (1993). The neural correlates of the verbal component of working memory. *Nature* 362: 342–5.

Pennington BF (1991). *Diagnosing Learning Disorders*. New York: Guilford Press.

Rourke BP, Feurst DR (1991). *Learning Disabilities and Psychosocial Functioning: A Neuropsychological Perspective*. New York: Guilford Press.

Rudel RG (1985). The definition of dyslexia: Language and motor deficits. In FH Duffy, N Geschwind (Eds), *Dyslexia: A Neuroscientific Approach to Clinical Evaluation*. Boston: Little Brown & Co.

Siegel LS (1989). IQ is irrelevant to the definition of learning disabilities. *Journal of Learning Disabilities* 22: 469–79.

Snowling MJ, Goulandris N, Bowlby M, Howell P (1986). Segmentation and speech perception in relation to reading skill: a developmental analysis. *Journal of Experimental Child Psychology* 41: 487–507.

Stanovich KE (1986). Matthew effects in reading: Some consequences of individual differences in the acquisition of literacy. *Reading Research Quarterly* 21: 360–407.

Stanovich KE (1988). The right and wrong places to look for the cognitive locus of reading disability. *Annals of Dyslexia* 38: 154–77.

Stanovich KE, Jacob RG, West RF, Vala-Rossi M (1985). Children's word recognition in context: Spreading activation, expectancy and modularity. *Child Development* 56: 1418–29.

Strag G (1972). Comparative behavioural ratings of parents with severely mentally retarded, special learning disability, and normal children. *Journal of Learning Disabilities* 5: 52–6.

Tallal P, Piercy M (1974). Developmental aphasia, rate of auditory processing and selective impairment of consonant perception. *Neuropsychologia* 12: 83–93.

Thomson ME (1984). *Developmental Dyslexia: Its Nature, Assessment and Remediation*. London: Edward Arnold.

Vellutino FR (1979). *Dyslexia: Theory and Research*. Cambridge, MA: MIT Press.

Wechsler D (1976). *Wechsler Intelligence Scale for Children – Revised (WISC-R)*. Windsor, Berks: NFER.

Wechsler D (1986). *Manual for the Wechsler Adult Intelligence Scale*, Revised UK edition. Sidcup, Kent: The Psychological Corporation.

West TG (1991). *In the Mind's Eye*. Buffalo, NY: Prometheus.

Wolf M (1991). Naming speed and reading: The contribution of the cognitive neurosciences. *Reading Research Quarterly* 26: 123–41.

Wright-Strawderman C, Watson BL (1992). The prevalence of depressive symptoms in children with learning disabilities. *Journal of Learning Disabilities* 25: 258–65.

Chapter 3
Stress factors in early education

PATIENCE THOMSON

A measure of stress in life is almost certainly unavoidable and can indeed even be welcome, if it is manageable. It is associated with challenge, with variations from routines which might otherwise become boring, with experiments and new initiatives. It is common to feel anxious when confronted with tests or examinations; yet we still seek qualifications. Considerable stress is involved during the initial period of ineptitude when learning a new sport, but we do not hesitate to do so. It is natural for many individuals to be competitive and ambitious; this necessarily involves stress.

Stress appears threatening only when it becomes pervasive and invasive, when it affects too many areas of our lives and when we have neither the strategies nor the energy to cope with it. With adults, high and undesirable levels of stress can be triggered by insecure social relationships, by a job that is unsuitable or too demanding, or by fear of unemployment, financial worries, uncertainty or failure. We also become stressed when the tasks required of us in our daily lives take an inordinate amount of time to accomplish, are ill-defined or are indeed impossible for us because either physically or mentally we do not have the right tools. A combination of too many of these factors can lead to an overwhelming sense of apprehension, incompetence and confusion, to lassitude, sleeplessness and fatigue. It also invites the victim to resort to escape mechanisms which indirectly relieve pressure, to fantasy, obsession, rebellion or withdrawal.

Undoubtedly, some individuals are able to cope with stress better than others. There are personality factors involved, but stress management is also a skill that can be learnt. It would be as impossible to protect children from a degree of stress as it would be unwise, because learning to recognise and control it is a necessary tool for survival in adult life. It is the task of parents and teachers and a very necessary part of education to prepare children for stress and to show them how to cope with it. It is also important that levels of stress should be monitored and controlled.

This is sometimes difficult in the case of the dyslexic child, when causes of stress may easily be underestimated or misinterpreted, so that the child is not taught correct strategies. It is quite likely that neither he nor his mentors will understand the nature and implications of his specific learning difficulties, or know how to relieve the accumulating stress that these are causing. This is often particularly true in the early years, before a professional diagnosis has been made. The dyslexic will also not be exempt from all the natural anxieties inherent for any child in the educational and maturational process. If stress levels become intolerably high, many dyslexic children develop their own inappropriate strategies, becoming disruptive, aggressive, withdrawn or school phobic. There is also evidence that children with special educational needs are less socially confident and more likely than their peers to be bullied in mainstream schools (Thompson et al., 1994).

Every child entering primary school is naturally subject to a degree of stress. There is likely to be some measure of separation anxiety at parting from his or her mother, at being released into a new environment for a considerable period of time daily, among strangers, in unfamiliar surroundings and in a social situation where there is no privacy or possibility of physical withdrawal. Under these circumstances many children take some time to adjust and to gain the confidence which comes from adapting to the school routine, mastering the elements of the working day and reacting appropriately to adults and peer group.

The normal difficulties of adjustment which face any child are compounded for the dyslexic because of certain inherent weaknesses. In the past, when dyslexia was regarded primarily as the persistent failure to learn to read and write, the natural assumption was that dyslexics would enter primary school with equal confidence and competence to other children. These, it was thought, would be eroded only when they were faced with formal academic tasks. However, more recent evidence suggests that the problems of the dyslexic child begin in the preschool era and that he will enter primary school vulnerable, if not positively disadvantaged.

Dyslexics will, by definition, have some if not all of a range of difficulties, which will affect their reactions and performance throughout their school career (Miles, 1993). There can be problems with the recording of information which is visually presented, particularly in relation to symbols, or difficulty with the correct sequential arrangement of such material. A dyslexic child may transpose letters within a word, writing 'taek' for 'take', or even the words themselves as in 'he come will'. Similarly digits in the answer to a sum may be reversed, and 16 becomes 61. Indeed confused directionality and lack of spatial awareness is a particular hindrance in mathematics where, for example, division sums start on the left and move to the right, whereas the right-hand column of figures must always be tackled first in an addition sum. Concepts of 'top' and 'bottom', 'above' and 'below' may also confuse. Many dyslexic children, in subtraction, will arbitrarily take away the top line from the bottom or vice versa as convenient, so that the answer to 74 minus 15 becomes 61. Fractions are particularly confusing. Incorrect orientation when writing digits can also give rise to errors, if for instance 5 is written as and interpreted as 3, just as 'b's' and 'd's' are confused when the child is reading or writing.

In the speech and language areas there will, in many cases, be problems with receptive and expressive language, evidenced by low scores on the British Picture Vocabulary Scales (Dunn and Dunn, 1982), the Test for Reception of Grammar (Bishop, 1983), the Renfrew Word-Finding Vocabulary Scale (Renfrew, 1988a) and the Renfrew Action Picture Test (Renfrew, 1988b). Lack of phonological awareness is common in dyslexic children and is a distinct handicap. Weak auditory blending, poor auditory discrimination and the inability to screen out irrelevant noise or identify accurately sound sequences hamper the effective processing of information presented through the auditory channel. Dyslexic children may also have naming problems which create considerable difficulties when information has to be stored in long-term memory and even greater ones when it has to be retrieved. Dockrell and McShane (1993) wrote that 'The most likely source of the poor memory performance of children with reading difficulties is their already established difficulties in phonological processing' and again 'The working memory system includes a specialised phonological store in which verbal information is retained'. Significantly they go on to say:

> If a printed word cannot be converted into sounds then its sounds cannot be stored; if conversion is slow, then previous sounds may be lost before further processing can occur; if the store is reduced in capacity, then the information cannot be retained; if the stored sounds cannot be blended, then a pronounceable form of the word cannot be obtained.

Dyslexic children are often caught up in a vicious circle. This is particularly true of reading. Bryant and Bradley (1985) point out that 'the child who learns to read is constantly exercising his memory'. They suggest that the poor memory scores of the unsuccessful reader 'could just as well be the result as the source of the failure to learn to read'. Muter (1994) suggests that phonological awareness is a powerful predictor of progress in beginning reading. She stresses, quoting Adams (1990), that the ability to segment words into their constituent phonemes or syllables, to blend sounds, to recognise rhymes and to manipulate phonemes by adding, deleting or transposing them are all good predictors of success in acquiring reading and spelling skills. If her evidence is borne in mind, it must follow that the dyslexic, lacking phonological awareness to such an extent that he cannot establish a foundation from which to develop even basic literacy skills, let alone refine them, falls further behind in his efforts to master those very reading skills which could improve his phonological skills and develop both memory and comprehension through practice and experience.

In the same way a child learns to craft words, sentences and paragraphs or to organise and structure his ideas through the very act of writing. If he has such technical problems with spelling, word retrieval or even handwriting that any written work is laborious and demoralising, then his skills will only improve at an agonisingly slow rate. A vicious circle is again created. Frustration builds up and, because there seems to be no satisfactory solution, stress accumulates. Impaired motor skills, both fine and gross, are also comparatively common with dyslexic children. Problems with fine motor control will prevent the accurate formation of letters and impede the recognition of patterns in words. If the physical act of writing is tiring, the child will probably attempt to reduce the task to a minimum.

In some cases hyperactivity or attention deficit disorder may further affect the child's performance and then the outlook can appear bleak indeed. These difficulties do not develop during the children's school career, but are often constitutional in origin and present a significant handicap from the affected child's first day in primary school and even long before.

A reception class child is soon expected to copy numbers, shapes and forms, and gradually to remember them with increasing accuracy and speed. Whereas other children will quickly learn to raise from memory a useful store of information which automatically relates sound to symbol and word to meaning, the dyslexic will search in vain for a key to past learning experience and fail to make the vital linkages. Visual and auditory stimuli need to be competently processed, often by linguistic means, to acquire basic literacy and numeracy skills.

Many dyslexics experience problems in the area of speech and language. Unfortunately for them, efficient and well-developed listening skills and competent information processing are vital prerequisites for successful accommodation to the school environment. The dyslexic child whose receptive language is vulnerable is disadvantaged throughout his working day. From the moment any child enters primary school, most instructions and explanations, praise and admonishment will be given verbally. Effective oral communication between teacher and pupil will depend on that child's ability to interpret language and to respond appropriately.

The dyslexic child may well process what is said to him individually, or to the class, slowly and inefficiently, and his difficulties will be greatly compounded by the distractions going on around him. He may well not be able to screen out irrelevant background noise, as a child without his difficulties would normally do. Sounds within and outside the classroom will divert his attention. He cannot automatically focus on the essentials of what he is being told, but may fasten on unimportant or random detail. If, as is likely, he has poor phonological awareness leading to slow and inaccurate processing of the spoken language, he will be confused about precise instructions, which he will quickly forget, and be reliant upon copying others if he is to accomplish the task that has been set. Anxiety and ensuing tiredness will impede concentration and lead to even more ineffective information processing. The exhausted child may well 'switch off'.

These problems with receptive language may also affect a dyslexic child's ability to participate in classroom discussion. He will be slower to process questions in comparison with the other children who will quickly have supplied correct answers which, given time, he might well have produced. His discouragement and frustration grow, confidence diminishes and motivation is reduced.

An informed teacher could mitigate the dyslexic's difficulties by placing him in the front of the class, by repeating instructions or even by 'buddying' him up with another friendly child who could prompt him when necessary. It is even possible to ensure that the dyslexic has extra time without interruption from others to answer questions. But to make such concessions, specific learning difficulties must have been recognised. Unless the teacher is exceptionally knowledgeable or perspicacious, or the parents particularly alert and well informed, it is unlikely that dyslexia will be diagnosed during the first or even the second year of formal schooling. It is more likely that the dyslexic child will be regarded as not particularly bright or as having emotional difficulties. This view will be confirmed when he is slow to acquire basic literacy and numeracy skills. Even when the teacher is sympathetic and helpful, the dyslexic child may be humiliated by the modified programme devised for him.

If receptive language is impaired, expressive language and communication skills are equally vulnerable. Dyslexic children often have word-finding or naming difficulties, which lead to circumlocution or vague and inaccurate statements. On the surface they may appear articulate, but close analysis of the content of their oral communication leads to the conclusion that they often repeat themselves, miss the point or fail to take account of the reaction of the listener. This develops into a social problem when they bore or mystify their audience, particularly other children who have neither the patience nor the inclination to tease out the thread of a story or argument from the dyslexic's confused attempts to express his ideas clearly.

Inadequate communication skills are as much a social as an academic disadvantage at every stage of school life. The dyslexic, struggling to make sense of the conversation of others, to frame his own interventions and to follow the train of thought, often fails to appreciate or even notice body language, facial expression or tone of voice. He fails to anticipate reactions, does not realise that he is inviting anger or criticism, and is aggrieved at the response he receives because he has not recognised the warning signs. Complaints that the dyslexic is often inappropriate in his language or comments are not confined to school and can equally lead to trouble and misunderstandings at home with parents, with siblings and with the extended family. If dyslexics are going to have problems with making friends in the playground or with social interaction with adults and their peers, these often start in the early years at primary school. They cannot therefore be entirely ascribed to the frustrations and emotional disturbances of school failure.

There is another contributory factor for many dyslexic children which often affects social relationships from a very early age. The whole area of motor difficulty as part of the broader dyslexic syndrome has aroused increasing interest and attention over the last few years. Many dyslexics experience problems with either gross or fine motor control, or both. Some of these problems are often referred to under the general heading of 'dyspraxia', particularly by parents who claim that the significance of these particular difficulties goes unrecognised and that no adequate support is forthcoming. Difficulties with gross motor control have obvious repercussions in school life. The child may have difficulties with eye–hand or eye–foot coordination, being unable to catch or kick a ball, a real disadvantage in the playground or on the sports field. In both games and physical education lessons a whole spectrum of difficulty is revealed, because often dyslexics can neither remember nor interpret instructions as a result of of their fallible receptive language skills, or follow them because of weak motor skills. In physical education lessons their lack of coordination and poor balance can make them look ridiculous when they try to hop, skip or walk a balance beam; in games erratic orientation, uncertain body image and left–right confusion mean that they turn the wrong way, run in the wrong direction, shoot 'own goals' (particularly after half-time) and generally appear to make fools of themselves. They are a liability in any team and often last to be selected. No wonder that many dyslexics choose to play the class clown and capitalise on their very weaknesses to attract attention, even if their behaviour attracts criticism or ridicule. Nor do the child's problems end with the formal physical education, swimming or games lessons. Limited time is scheduled for the children to change for the next period. Dyslexic children who display typical symptoms of dyspraxia may struggle with buttons and shoe-laces or put on their clothes in the wrong order. They will often take an inordinately long time to dress themselves while the rest of the class and teacher wait impatiently.

Motor difficulties will be apparent in class, when the dyspraxic child clumsily brushes the jar of pencils off the teacher's desk, knocks over the paint-pot or jolts the desks of other children, to their considerable annoyance. He cannot stand quietly in line, but will jostle others who naturally push and shove back. If he has poor muscle tone he will slouch uncomfortably at his desk, wriggle on his seat and distract himself and others by his restlessness.

Problems with fine motor control, even before serious handwriting is required, affect dyslexic children's ability to draw or colour efficiently within the lines. Often they will use undue pressure and their hand will quickly tire; growing frustration that they are not succeeding at the set task will compound the situation and they will give up. All fine motor tasks will present problems as, for instance, those associated with early learning in mathematics such as the manipulation of concrete aids, the counting of beads or the measuring and matching of blocks. What for other children is a task that can be accomplished with practised ease and manual dexterity, while retaining the overall concept of what they are trying to do, becomes for the dyslexic a complicated procedure where each step presents a challenge. As in the early stages of riding a bicycle, when to proceed too slowly is constantly to fall off, the dyslexic child is deprived of the impetus which carries the whole exercise forward to a satisfactory conclusion. In the context of fine motor control it is also worth mentioning that a few of the younger dyslexic children have difficulty in chewing their food and the slowness of their mastication creates problems at dinner-time, when their plateful is half-eaten as others are clearing away. They may want their food mashed or minced. This may be one of the reasons why they are sometimes 'fussy eaters', and invite adverse comment from unsympathetic adults.

The catalogue of dyslexic vulnerability is not yet complete. A large proportion of dyslexics seem lost in both space and time and this has serious implications which militate against confident survival in the school environment. Many adults will have experienced the confusion and frustration of asking for directions in a foreign city with little or no knowledge of the native language. Traffic appears to approach from the wrong direction, landmarks are unfamiliar and the bustling, purposeful crowd is seemingly unwilling to pause to give help or instructions. If people do oblige they often talk too fast and create further embarrassment. The dyslexic constantly experiences similar anxiety throughout the normal school day. Most children quickly pick up the geography of a new school environment. The whereabouts of cloakroom, toilets, classroom and hall are soon established. In contrast the dyslexic is slow to prepare for the next move, follows on behind the rest of his class, is left behind and finds himself lost, worried and confused.

Similarly there is an inaccurate conception of time. The dyslexic has no intuitive recognition of time past, time present or time future. He may turn up late or early for a lesson, will greatly over- or underestimate the time required for any given task, will be muddled not only as to the day of the week but as to the time of day. One 7-year-old dyslexic claimed that there was no order to the days of the week, that the holidays were comprised entirely of Saturdays and Sundays and that a whole school week could consist entirely of Mondays. When asked how he could tell which day of the week it was, he said you could usually guess from the teacher's face. No wonder such children, unless their parents are vigilant, fail to bring in their football gear or swimming trunks on the correct day and hence get themselves into trouble. An 11-year-old dyslexic who was asked the date of her birthday was embarrassed and appeared not to know. 'When was it last year?' 'July 15th.' The teacher could not control the hilarity with which this statement was greeted by the other children. The girl had obviously not grasped the concept that her birthday was on the same day every year. One day I re-scheduled a weekly religious education period from the last period in the day to the session before lunch. At the end of the period the entire class of dyslexic children picked up their bags and proceeded to go to the cloakroom, ready to go home, without any sense that it was still only midday. I have often observed a dyslexic child in a craft, design and technology or computer lesson completely absorbed in a task and quite unaware that the hour was up and the bell had gone. When recalled, he was aggrieved and angry, resenting the intrusive need for transferral of attention dictated by a seemingly inexorable and intrusive school routine.

Such sudden focusing of attention in the otherwise distractible dyslexic child, this almost obsessive determination to hang on to any area where success is possible, leads on to discussion of that major cause of stress for the dyslexic, frustration. It lies within the very definition of specific learning difficulties that there are pronounced areas of difficulty and vulnerability, but also areas of considerable strength. This distinguishes the dyslexic child from the child with moderate or severe learning difficulties who is globally affected. There is a wide range of IQs among dyslexics, as with any other children. Unlike other children, those with the higher IQs do not necessarily have a better prognosis in terms of academic success. Indeed their failure to acquire the basic literacy and numeracy skills, essential for academic progress, usually leaves the brighter child more inclined to adverse emotional reactions, which further block his capacity to learn. The inability to capitalise on potential, to express individual ideas concisely, to tell inventive stories plausibly or, to communicate original concepts is a major cause of stress.

I have detailed a number of areas within the primary school day where the dyslexic child is likely to feel underconfident, threatened and incompetent. Against this background it is understandable that stress can soon reach disproportionate levels, as the child struggles to achieve in situations where, because of the nature of his specific difficulties, he is seriously disadvantaged. There are too few windows of opportunity when he has a chance to shine, to relax and to redeem his reputation.

From the moment dyslexic children first enter primary school, they are often a source of puzzlement to their teachers. To brand them as lazy or stupid seems inappropriate, yet their failures in so many areas reduce expectations and the teacher may increasingly assign them less demanding tasks, hoping to preserve their morale. The unfortunate consequence can be that the dyslexic child who is not challenged may cease to set himself high standards. Low expectations invite low performance. Yet such children are still often aware that they are not truly unintelligent and the contrast between their potential and their performance inevitably gives rise to stress.

Apparent failure at school does not pass unnoticed by the parents, who start to become anxious. In their turn they too are confused. Often there was little concrete evidence before their child started at primary school that anything was amiss. Some clumsiness, a quaint way with words or failure to remember instructions could easily be ascribed to general immaturity. The parents' increasing worries reflect on the child. If there are other siblings without learning difficulties the parents may be tactful enough not to make direct comparisons, but the child will usually be aware of the discrepancies. A deep sense of unease begins to grow as the child becomes conscious that he is disappointing his family. Stress for the dyslexic is not confined to school but permeates home life as well. As it grows it can lead to such manifestations of emotional disturbance as temper tantrums, aggression and bed wetting. An element of guilt may be set up in either child or parents, whose management of the child becomes increasingly uncertain. Pressure creates further stress, but acceptance of failure can appear to be demoralising patronage and a middle way is hard to find.

For parents or teachers of children who are not only dyslexic but are also hyperactive or have an attention deficit, and this is certainly a factor in a proportion of cases, the scene is even more complicated and the correct approach even more uncertain. Their difficulties have been concisely and comprehensively described by Barkley (1992). He explains the implications of attention deficit–hyperactivity disorder or ADHD. One of the significant problems is inconsistent work performance. The failure of ADHD children to stay on task, their impulsive behaviour, disorganisation and unpredictable reactions exhaust adults, annoy other children and impede constructive learning. Almost inevitably they attract negative reactions and will often respond with attention-seeking behaviour, which is unpopular in class and distressing in the home environment. Such children suffer because they are not invited home by others and can be partially ostracised at school, or teased and even bullied by exasperated peers.

This wide spectrum of difficulties extending into so many areas of the dyslexic child's life renders him extremely vulnerable to levels of stress which are unacceptable, inhibiting and even threatening. It is interesting to trace, through case histories, the different reactions of individuals to such stress and to consider how best it can be alleviated.

Until now, for convenience, dyslexic children have been referred to in this chapter as of masculine gender. However, I have, during my last 5 years as Principal of a school for 90 dyslexic children of primary school age, seen the number of girls grow from 12 to 30. The precise reasons for this increase are hard to define. The problems of dyslexic girls can appear on the surface to be subtly different from those of the boys and may emerge at a rather later stage. Some seem to learn to read reasonably efficiently, but for them this is a mechanical decoding exercise and their difficulties lie more in the area of information processing, comprehension and organisational skills – all factors of increasing importance in the later years at primary school. Problems with numeracy skills seem common in girls and are now more readily recognised as part of the pattern of dyslexic difficulty. I shall therefore include girls in my case studies. Pseudonyms will be used throughout.

Bruce

Bruce is the second child in a family of four. He was an early developer, learning to stand at 9 months and starting to talk at a year. He had no noticeable early articulation problems and his speech was apparently fluent, although his stories rambled, he could never remember names and his jokes missed the point. At almost 5 years of age, he started attending his local primary school. He seemed an active, cheerful, well-adjusted child, although somewhat accident prone, resulting in frequent trips to the local accident and emergency department. He badly burnt his hand stirring the bonfire with a metal rod and required stitches after a brawl with older children in the park. However, such incidents were ascribed to his impulsive behaviour, his fearlessness and his intense curiosity about the physical world around him. He entered a large reception class of over 40 children. His early failure to make any sort of start with learning to read or write was ascribed in part to lack of individual attention from the teacher in a large and somewhat undisciplined class.

During Bruce's second year at primary school it was suggested that he join a small remedial group. His mother was informed that he was 'not particularly bright' and needed extra help. Bruce was tall for his age and it was at this time that he began to team up with the tougher and rougher elements in his class; there was evidence that he was getting involved in fights in the playground. At home there were temper tantrums, threats to walk out (he would occasionally leave, reappearing somewhat sheepishly a couple of hours later), bed wetting and sibling rivalry. It did not help morale that his older brother was thriving at school and that his younger sister, still of preschool age, was a precocious learner. Bruce identified himself as the 'dim one' of the family.

In Bruce's third year at primary school his parents received a letter from his headmaster expressing considerable concern and suggesting that he be referred to the School Psychology Service. Comments on

Bruce's problems included the following:

> ... The need to sound out most of the words. [He appeared to retain very few of the 'look and say' words.]
> A habit of seizing on a particular letter in a word and guessing at a possible solution using the letter always as an initial one ...
> The reproduction of a word by indicating the framework, e.g. d l v for 'delivery'.

Bruce was not making progress, even in his small group remedial lessons. He was restless and inattentive in class, unable to stay on task and was distracting the other children.

The Local Authority Educational Psychologist confirmed the Headmaster's identification of Bruce's problems. She established that he was of above-average intelligence. It was subsequently agreed with the understanding and sympathetic Headmaster that his parents could take Bruce privately to an Educational Psychologist with a special interest in dyslexia. She pronounced Bruce's dyslexia to be severe and predicted serious behaviour problems unless specialised help was immediately forthcoming. Private tuition was arranged three times a week and Bruce made dramatic progress. His confidence increased and with it his motivation and attention span. As he learnt to read, it emerged that he was a competent mathematician. Failure to decode mathematical instructions had initially hampered his progress. At home he was calmer, better organised and more relaxed. He started to invite friends back from school and to play more naturally with his siblings.

Bruce's problems were not over yet and there would, in fact, be years of hard work and essential support ahead to ensure that he mastered the curriculum and did justice to himself in the necessary examinations that would enable him to move on through the succeeding stages of his academic career. However, because he was diagnosed early and appropriate help was forthcoming, teachers, parents and Bruce himself acquired the insight into his specific problem which enabled them to alleviate stress. Sympathetic and properly targeted treatment was forthcoming for his specific learning difficulties as they manifested themselves in different forms throughout his time at school. As was appropriate for an individual with an overall IQ of 128, Bruce eventually went to university.

Anne

Anne was less fortunate. Her problem went undiagnosed until she was a grown woman in her 20s. The following is a quotation from a letter (retaining her spelling) in which she describes her early experiences at primary school:

> So I would like to tell you about my school years. I think I was about seven years old when I became awair that I wasn't learning very much. My reading

was very poor untill I was about 11 years and my spelling was awful and my maths were poor. I remember I didn't know my left from my right hand and couldn't tell the time. We were taught these things as a class of thirty children and I seemed to be the only one who didn't learn. So when we had writing I always did a lovely picture and wrote 'This is . . .' or 'The something or other' in big letters to fill up the page. And I remember getting my 'b's' and 'd's' mixed up and so I became good at art and craft and didn't progress in spelling at all. So I was put in the D stream and that was that . . .

We had a nasty and old headmistress and she was the plague of my childhood she always picked me out and when I couldn't give the right answers she would shout at me and when she was angry she would spit the words at me. She always made me cry and I was so frightened of her. She tried to bully me into getting it right and I really wanted to please her She would hold flashcards up and i had to say the words that were written on them. One of the words were Doll and another Ball and I couldn't tell them apart. An so i would guess anf the other kids werld giggle and I knew I was in for it.

So I hated school I hated my tetchers because they were picking on me and I would tell them so in front of the class. I would accuse them of tearing my picture or of spoiling something I had made. And looking back they were nice everbody liked them exept me.

Particular points of interest in this letter are the evidence of considerable frustration, anger and aggression, the development of inappropriate avoidance strategies and the sense of isolation from other children. They responded naturally to the teacher and mastered with apparent ease even simple tasks which Anne herself found frustrating and impossible. Ridicule alienated her, sarcasm destroyed her confidence, and lack of sympathy or understanding further demoralised her. Anne's school days left her stressed and liable to periods of depression. She found it difficult to cope in adult life until, as a result of a chance meeting, she learnt about dyslexia and the pattern of her difficulties fell into place. She set about seeking help.

Kenneth and Terry

Anne was like many dyslexic children who develop avoidance strategies in the face of the undermining academic and social problems created by their specific learning difficulties. Kenneth, aged 9, simply refused to get up in the morning and lay like a dead weight in bed, equally impervious to bribes and threats. His mother could not dress him, feed him his breakfast or drag him to the school bus. Finally she gave up and waited for the school authorities to intervene. Terry went to school and attended Assembly but shortly afterwards would be stricken by stomach cramps. Pale and tearful he would wait to be collected by his reluctant father. Yet if his bluff was called and he was sent back to class he would, on occasion, be physically sick. Not until he received specific help and encouragement and academic progress had started did his genuine pains diminish and finally vanish.

Paul

Paul was 9 years old when he came to us and was a non-starter in reading. At his local primary school he had been the victim of much teasing. At first, when he found himself in an environment where his specific learning difficulties were recognised and remediation was at hand, his new-found confidence converted him into a bully and a rebel. No longer cowed, he threw his weight around. Two years' progress in reading within his first year converted his attitude and his behaviour became tolerable, although he remained wary and still found it difficult to react naturally to adults and his peers. Being less preoccupied with his problems and better able to concentrate on the task in hand he derived more satisfaction from lessons and was, emotionally, at last available for work.

Others

Edmund had great charm and a talent for 'creative ineptitude'. He avoided work by appearing constantly busy and attentive, but spent an inordinate amount of time drawing careful margins, sharpening pencils or volunteering to run errands.

Christopher, on the other hand, became withdrawn and sulky and was so quiet and unobtrusive that it was scarcely noticed when he skipped a lesson.

Sarah established on the first day of each new class that she was a non-performer, particularly in mathematics. She did this apologetically and with the warmest of smiles, pre-empting reproach and effectively limiting expectations.

Roger was rude and disruptive, making it clear to teacher and classmates that the reason for his academic failure lay in his rejection of the entire system.

Alison created a fantasy world for herself into which she retired when under pressure. Her absent expression was usually attributed to a failure to understand rather than lack of attention. The eventual establishment of an above-average IQ came as a great surprise to her teachers.

The problems that each of these attitudes presents to the teacher or parent are as nothing to the difficulties that face the individual concerned. All these strategies are only temporary measures for alleviating stress and anxiety. As the child progresses through primary school, the growing realisation of the increased pressure that awaits him at secondary school or even of the demands of the adult world begins to trouble him, and panic starts to take hold.

As lessons become more formalised and subject-oriented, the academic difficulties of the dyslexic become increasingly apparent. Problems with reading and comprehension, with language processing and sequential memory, with spelling and written work intrude more deeply. The older primary age child will be required to use reference books, to research projects, to take notes or extract information from written material. It will be hard for him to remember names in geography or history or sequential processes in scientific experiments.

Lawrence's mathematics are weak because his fine motor skills affect his ability to line up figures. John copies numbers inaccurately because of his weak visual discrimination. Tim still cannot decode mathematical questions of any complexity because his receptive language and reading skills are vulnerable. Michael has problems with orientation and confuses the signs. Their specific difficulties are different but failure is the common factor.

For children proceeding to private education, examinations and tests loom as a real threat. The time constraint here is a major factor, with slow language processing skills proving a handicap in revision and essay writing. Pauline, aged 11, wrote her essay on 'shells' instead of 'smells', having misread the question. Realising to her horror in the last 5 minutes what she had done, she hopefully wrote 'Shells have no smells' as her last sentence. Examinations are stressful for all individuals, but are partly a matter of confidence, and certainly require intense concentration. The additional problems that examinations present to dyslexics distract them and drain their confidence. This creates such anxiety and stress that under-performance is almost guaranteed.

Academic success, for the dyslexic, often depends on two vital factors. He must acquire literacy and numeracy skills at a level that will enable him to access information efficiently and express himself in written form. Equally important, self-esteem, motivation and confidence must be preserved because the dyslexic is almost certainly going to have to work harder than his peers to achieve his potential. Unless basic skills are taught before the child reaches secondary school, the gap between his level of ability and that of his peers will have widened to an extent where catching up will be an almost impossibly long and demoralising process. Strategies and skills must not only be taught but practised early if they are to become automatic and if a child is not to miss the foundation work which underpins the secondary curriculum.

Twenty years ago, when I became seriously involved in the field of dyslexia, I was working with maladjusted and delinquent boys in their late teens. All were of above-average intelligence. I taught them in groups and, twice a week, on an individual basis. My remit was to ensure that they learnt the basic literacy and numeracy skills which they had failed to learn at primary school. Attendance at my lessons was mandatory. Using skills I had learnt in the Dyslexic Clinic of St Bartholomew's Hospital in London, under the direction of Dr Beve Hornsby, it was possible in almost every case to develop these boys' literacy and numeracy skills to a level where they could cope with the everyday demands of adult life and of a simple manual job. Looking back over the often well-documented school records of these boys, it was apparent that problems had already begun at primary school level with manifestations of specific learning difficulties which had hindered academic progress. They had entered secondary school as virtual non-starters. Problems of truancy and non-cooperation created a climate where it was easy to slip into anti-social or delinquent habits. Alleviation of stress at an early age through appropriate teaching and more resources allocated for support at primary school could well have pre-empted these much more serious social problems from developing.

The parents of the primary school-age children in my school often ask such questions as 'Is there a cure for dyslexia?' or 'How long will it take for my child to get over his specific learning difficulties?'. The answer can only be that dyslexia is endemic, may be genetic or neurological in origin, and there is no magic cure. There will always be areas that are potentially stressful if they demand precisely the skills and expertise most difficult for the dyslexic to master. However, there are successful strategies, which can be taught, which vastly improve the capacity to communicate efficiently, to process information, to develop organisational and study skills, and thus to fulfil potential. Modified teaching styles employed by those specifically trained to recognise and remediate specific learning difficulties, and carefully structured and adapted programmes, enable dyslexic children to acquire the necessary basic literacy and numeracy skills to access the school curriculum. It must not be forgotten, however, that there is stress even in the remedial situation, because intense and prolonged effort will be required if the dyslexic is to 'catch up'.

There is a very fine line between stress that creates challenge and stress that inhibits and constitutes a handicap. The primary school dyslexic child who is taught to overcome his specific learning difficulties will gain thereby a strength and confidence which will enable him to cope with the later pressures of teenage and adult life. The dyslexic child who fails to obtain crucial support in the early stages may well succumb to levels of stress which he can neither control nor understand, which undermine motivation and shatter confidence. He may opt out, with disastrous consequences not only for his educational development but for his future prospects reaching far into adult life.

The last word can most appropriately come from the dyslexic child himself, in this case an intelligent 10 year old who had been sent to see me, the Principal, because he had kicked another child who had taunted him. I sat him down at my desk with a clean sheet of paper to put his side of the story:

> A blitixik I think can get angry a tierd of triyng in lessons and they might get
> there tenshon out on bullying or teasing but just so they can get their stress
> out, they might fell depresed or upset. They can also give up which is not the

thing to do as they can get traped in a bubble and do need help to get out of it. they need help and if any bodyknose a diletic they shod be their friend or cher them up there is no reson that a dislexic can not be treated like a normal person. They do need help in their work but they shod not be treated diferently.

References

Adams MJ (1990). *Beginning to Read – Thinking and Learning about Print*. Cambridge, MA: MIT Press.

Barkley RA (1992). *ADHD. What Can We Do?* New York: Guilford Press.

Bishop DVM (1983). *Test for Reception of Grammar*. Available from the author, MRC Applied Psychology Unit, 15 Chaucer Road, Cambridge.

Bryant P, Bradley, L (1985). *Children's Reading Problems*. Oxford: Blackwell.

Dockrell J, McShane J (1993). *Children's Learning Difficulties*. Oxford: Blackwell.

Dunn, LM, Dunn LM (1982). *British Picture Vocabulary Scale*. Windsor: NFER-Nelson.

Miles TR (1993). *Dyslexia: The Pattern of Difficulties*, 2nd edn. London: Whurr.

Muter V (1994). Influence of phonological awareness and letter knowledge on beginning reading and spelling development. In C Hulme, M Snowling (Eds), *Reading Development and Dyslexia*. London: Whurr.

Renfrew CE (1988a). *Word-Finding Vocabulary Scale*. Oxford: Renfrew.

Renfrew CE (1988b). *Action Picture Test*. Oxford: Renfrew.

Thompson D, Whitney I, Smith, P (1994). Bullying of children with special needs in mainstream schools. *Support for Learning* 3: 103–6.

Chapter 4
Stress factors in the adolescent

S.J. CHINN and MARYROSE CROSSMAN

Introduction

We work in a school for dyslexic adolescent boys. In this chapter we record some of the signs of stress that we have observed in our pupils and some of the main things that we have tried to do to help. Obviously the responses to stress vary considerably from one dyslexic individual to another, but this does not preclude the possibility of tentative generalisation.

Academic stresses

Most of our students have been keen to do well academically, but this of itself can sometimes create stress. Presented here are some of their accounts of situations that they find stressful:

> When I don't understand and the teacher gives you another explanation and I sense the teacher is getting up-tight.

> If I know I should be able to spell an easy word and I can't get it out.

> If I have a good idea in CDT [craft, design and technology] and it costs too much or I don't have enough time.

> If I don't get help when I ask for it.

> If I am singled out in class.

> When there is more work to do than there is time to do it in.

> When others boast about their work.

It is possible that, as adults, we do not always appreciate the subtlety of the reasons that lead to stress. One pupil said to us:

> I get stressed when I have failed and people say, 'Never mind, you did your best'. I don't want to fail when I have done my best. If I think I am going to fail then I won't do my best so when I do fail I can think, 'Well, I didn't try'.

Another source of stress is the difficulty that some dyslexics experience in trying to 'find the right word'. They may often be in situations where they have what they know to be good ideas and yet find themselves unable to communicate them to others – let alone write them on paper.

Finally, there is the widespread problem of stress over written examinations. We are not, of course, suggesting that dyslexics are the only people who feel stress when examinations are approaching. However, their unusual balance of skills puts them at much more risk. They are in effect being asked to operate via a medium (the written word) that does not come at all easily to them; they may well feel that they know the subject but find great difficulty in expressing their knowledge on paper. We have had particular experience of the GCSE examinations and we have found that GCSE-induced stress can make itself felt a long time before the actual examination. The recent loss of the 100% coursework option for GCSE English has been a great blow to many of our students. They need to feel that our support – at a time when one might have expected them to prefer independence – is overtly apparent for revision and preparation.

Social stresses

It seems clear that many dyslexics are disadvantaged from an early age because of misperceptions, misjudgements and misreadings within the social sphere. The situation is sometimes compounded if they come from families where there are other dyslexics, because then opportunities for misunderstanding are multiplied. In particular, linguistic communication is affected: words are liable to be misunderstood, and other people's remarks may be seen as threatening or teasing when they were not intended to be anything of the kind.

Moreover, just as most dyslexics have difficulty in reading print and learn to do so only after a large amount of individual tuition, so in a similar fashion they may not spontaneously learn to 'read' body language, and could therefore be unaware of the information that can be gained from eye contact or from the observation of other people's bodily movements; as a consequence they may fail to respond suitably.

There are situations in which, with the best of intentions, dyslexics behave in socially inappropriate ways. On one occasion, one of the authors (MC) was sitting with her husband in a café. She writes as follows:

> It was a wet day; but before we had spread our coats on the chair backs – that is, before we were even seated – the proprietress was there, standing closely over us and thrusting out two menus. Within 5 minutes she was back, saying 'What do you want?'. My sandwiches came nearly 10 minutes before my husband's cooked meal (not uncommon, I admit) and without cutlery.

Looking round I could see that 'sandwiches equals fingers' regardless of filling! As we finished madame reappeared, booming 'What more do you want?'. The bill came promptly and was paid to madame's husband, who asked, 'Was it all right?'. This experience struck me as so dyslexic – the willingness was there but the awareness was not, while the verbal communication and the body language were skewed. (In passing, what about my dyslexic colleague who was finding it quite hard to eat a bowl of custard and wondering why. Was it possibly because she was using a fork?)

Both at home and at school the physical appearance of the adolescent may cause stressful interactions with parents and teachers. Sometimes, of course, this is simply a manifestation of teenage rebellion, because an obvious way of displaying independence is by adopting particular styles of dress or hair. In addition, however, we have found a number of dyslexics who – with no wish to be 'rebellious' – were particularly inept at choosing appropriate clothing. Some of them had difficulty in mixing and matching colour and pattern, whereas others seemed unaware of what clothes were suitable for a particular occasion. In these cases adverse reactions from their peers was a further source of stress.

We make a point of encouraging personal hygiene. This means praising those whose hair looks clean, shiny and well kept. We have been known to buy shampoo, deodorant and the like, and in a lighthearted way we encourage regular changes of underwear! Sometimes we assist in the choosing of clothes. Many teenagers are adamant about what they will/will not wear, but it may be possible to guide them a little or discuss what style of clothing is suitable for a given occasion. For instance, one can discuss what is 'smart casual', i.e. right for a theatre trip, what will be adequate for an outing to the coast, what to wear for a presentation or for a visit to a farm, when trainers will do and when 'proper' shoes are needed, and so on. We have found that there are some dyslexics who are teased by their peers because of their odd appearance or because they are wearing inappropriate clothes.

Approaches to members of the other sex are of course difficult enough for any adolescent, but for the dyslexic there is extra uncertainty because of his difficulty in recognising verbal and non-verbal cues. Credibility is not enhanced, of course, if he is a poor reader or a poor writer of letters.

In some cases there may be additional pressure from parents. If they are anxious for their child to succeed there is a risk that they may become over-demanding; and even those who start by saying that 'all they want is for the child to be happy' may sometimes increase their expectations beyond what is reasonable. Often the areas of schooling where academic success is available for students centre on literacy skills, examinations and memory. These are the very areas where dyslexics are disadvantaged.

There are, of course, sources of stress for the adolescent which are not primarily the result of dyslexia. The move into secondary education may affect some pupils more than others; for example, there may be 'new class mates, new teachers and new sets of rules . . . also for many of them a violation of their expectations' (Lacey, 1971, p.161). Stresses may sometimes give rise to migraines, abdominal pains and the like, and in some cases there may be aggressive behaviour, glumness, even thumb-sucking. There are further sources of stress if an adolescent has to cope with the deaths of grandparents or friends, the latter increasingly possible because of drug-related fatalities, AIDS and road accidents. None of these is the direct consequence of dyslexia but if the person who experiences them is also dyslexic this may compound his problems.

Ways of helping

For adults who deal with dyslexic teenagers the key requirements are sensitivity and understanding. If there is awareness of the factors that lead to stress then commonsense will suggest ways of responding. A sense of humour is particularly valuable and tense situations can sometimes be defused by laughter. It is in no way surprising that many dyslexics should feel under stress at examination times or have a general lack of confidence in themselves. What is important is that the adults should understand this and be able to combine realism and encouragement. They should remember, too, that they themselves are not exempt from feeling stresses and anxieties, and there is no reason why, in suitable circumstances, this should not be discussed with the pupils. As was pointed out earlier, one of our pupils reported that he could 'sense the teacher is getting up-tight'.

Differences in temperament mean that we can expect our adolescents to respond differently to similar stresses as they search for their roles in life. Some of them (with so-called 'extrovert' personality) may appear to cope well with experiences and to handle information and social situations quite competently, but they may also react impulsively and with little consideration of longer-term consequences. The quieter or more timid youngster may perceive his world as threatening, and take longer to emerge and tackle new situations with confidence and be less ready to take risks. In both cases adults living and working alongside need to concentrate on increasing the teenager's awareness of self-worth. This is a thread running through every area of stress; positive perceptions of self-esteem are perhaps the greatest treasure a young person can be given, and they need to be built in from a very early stage and to be constantly reinforced.

Sadly many teenagers reach puberty with very poor perceptions of their own value. Those who are dyslexic may have become discouraged and despondent through repeated perceived (and often real) failure – at school or at home or, worse, both. The task of teachers is to repair the existing damage, to prevent it from increasing further, and above all to encourage an attitude of 'thinking positive'. They need to bear in mind that a teenager may be acting out on one occasion and behaving like a mature adult soon after.

Listening is an important social skill and failure to listen is something that can be explicitly discussed. For example, if we are in the process of explaining something to a pupil and he interrupts, we have found that the best procedure is to stop talking – to wait until the silence sinks in and the pupil looks at you again. You can then explain why you stopped – and carry on with your point without waiting for his excuse or distracting comment. Eventually your sudden silence will suffice and no explanation will be needed. If he starts to interrupt but stops himself, signal with a smile or a touch that you are pleased and carry on. Then do him the courtesy of being an active listener yourself, so that he is rewarded and learns the subtle body language that signals to him that you, the listener, are hearing and appreciating him, the speaker. These include nods, eye contact, a smile, an occasional quiet 'mphm'.

It is always our policy to stop the teenager who barges through doors, who walks between two people holding a conversation, who leans across others at the table, or who helps himself and ignores others. But we explain why we are doing so – and if possible inject some humour into the explanation.

Dyslexics are very liable to misread emotions expressed facially – and to get into trouble as a consequence. Frowns of puzzlement and frowns of disapproval are different, but it takes a degree of social sophistication to recognise this. Some children are so accustomed to 'being in trouble' that they tend frequently to interpret most facial expressions as disapproval unless there are obvious manifestations of joy and surprise. Joy and surprise are themselves frequently confused. Smaller children can be helped if one draws faces on cards, with the appropriate emotion written on each, and these give opportunities for chat, story-telling and even pulling your own faces! However, this is not something that teenagers appreciate. In their case cartoons or illustrated stories may be useful, in which the emotional states of the characters can be inferred. If they misinterpret such expressions they can be asked to demonstrate the emotion that they themselves thought was there.

Eye contact can also be practised. In our culture a person who looks away may be thought rude, as may a person who talks not to the listener but to a wall or ceiling. Conversely, however, it is also rude to 'stare'. We have found it is possible to keep prompting the child to look in one's direction; one can smile when he does and even joke about the fact that one does not like 'talking to a brick wall'.

Social skills can also be learned from members of the pupil's peer group, for example, if they play competitive games such as monopoly.

Some dyslexics may be unsure 'whose turn it is', and in these sorts of game they can learn to share, to accept defeat – and to accept praise – which is a welcome change for those who for years have been accustomed to a 'failure' label.

Those who find social interactions dangerous or painful may try to take refuge in a safe formula that can be 'trotted out' on all occasions (such as 'How are you these days?'). The difficulty here is that if they persist with it they may find themselves rebuffed or laughed at. We have had boys who, when first with us, will say 'hello' to the same staff member *every* time they meet – or say 'Have a nice day' even though it is evening! These are genuine efforts to engage in social interaction but they fail because the actions are routine rather than spontaneous. It is important that the staff member should not reinforce this kind of behaviour. It is possible to give a friendly response while at the same time expressing some degree of surprise at the repetition. If there is time one can sometimes explain this surprise, so that instead of the stock phrase there is genuine dialogue.

In a classroom it is possible to encourage role-playing. One can set up social situations and apportion personalities or types to the different members of the class. How does an outsider break into a socially thriving group? How can members of a group combine most effectively to solve a problem? Different routes to a stated goal can be discussed, and if responses are inappropriate the teacher can help the pupils to recognise that this is the case.

A possible response to stress is, of course, to be aggressive. We have had few pupils whose aggression actually led them into delinquency, but we know of some who would almost certainly have fallen foul of the law without our intervention. Many others have behaved aggressively at times, and we have tried to make clear that this is unacceptable while at the same time allowing them to keep their self-respect.

As is always our principle, our reactions to and perceptions of each student must be individualised, but we hope that they are based on the experience that we have gained and continue to gain as we work with different individuals.

Reference

Lacey C (1971). In Cashdan A, Whitehead J (Eds), *Personality, Growth and Learning*. London: Oxford University Press.

Chapter 5
Stress factors in the college student

DOROTHY GILROY

The personal counselling element in study skills teaching

This chapter is based on experiences of working with over 150 under-graduates, assessed as dyslexic, who have been given academic and personal support by the Dyslexia Unit at the University of Wales, Bangor, since work with undergraduates was established on a formal basis in 1978. (For a description of this work, see Gilroy, 1991.) The student service was originally set up when, as a language-trained tutor, I was appointed to help six students with study skills, particularly essay writing. The service was seen principally in terms of academic support and there was perhaps the underlying assumption that because these students had 'made it' to university (quite an achievement for dyslexics in the 1970s) they would be fairly confident and able to cope. However, within the first year of its operation a strong need for personal counselling emerged; this need became evident as the relationship between the tutor and the students developed and the students felt able to express their personal anxieties. It became obvious that their feelings, attitudes and motivation were intertwined with the technical aspects of study: problems with study triggered off a whole pattern of anxiety and resurrected underlying insecurities which, in turn, further inhibited their ability to cope with their academic work. Our approach to study therefore has always considered the stress factors of the dyslexic student and treated him or her as a 'whole person', an approach that has been reinforced by Hales (1994) in a study entitled 'The human aspects of dyslexia' which indicates that over recent years researchers have realised that the personal and emotional element of dyslexia is more important than was previously acknowledged.

University students can be self-analytical, reflective and articulate; coming into in a new environment, they are also able to look retrospectively at their home and school experiences, and express their feelings

55

about them. Our first generation of dyslexic students taught us a great deal about the anxieties they had experienced in the past, and it became obvious that the balance of the relationship between personal stress and insecurity, and academic skill, had to be very carefully considered: with some students their stress was alleviated by setting to work immediately upon a language or study problem; with other students their stress inhibited their study and no real academic progress could be made until the student had started to come to terms with his or her personal emotions.

The specific difficulties of dyslexic students and their need for support may not be readily understood by mainstream subject tutors who do not know about dyslexia. They may argue that all students suffer from stress and indeed dyslexic students fit the general pattern of study stress revealed in Milner (1980), Raaheim and Wankowski (1981), or Peelo (1994). However, dyslexic students have a specific language disability which has perhaps caused them much difficulty in their earlier school career and which continues to make them more anxious and more prone to stress; so they develop the stress symptoms more quickly, experience them more deeply, and find greater difficulty coping with them because these stress symptoms, in turn, intensify the language and sequencing difficulties caused by dyslexia.

The service offered by the Dyslexia Unit involves study skills support, both in a group and individually, personal counselling, and help with claiming the Disabled Students' Allowance. In general, registration with and attendance at the Dyslexia Unit are voluntary, although over the years of its existence five students have been admitted to the university on condition that they attend the Unit sessions. Approximately 15%, although being aware of the service, have turned to it only in moments of crisis (a typical comment on the 1994 service evaluation was: 'I did not come in very often, but I always knew that you were there to turn to.').

When they are stressed, the students 'turn to us' in various ways, perhaps deliberately chosen, or perhaps spontaneously seeking an answer to their need. Students who feel under stress and who need urgent personal counselling may in fact come during the set group period. For some of them this is the deliberate choice: they will be aware that there are other students present and they may, in fact, have chosen to share their problems with these others. On these occasions the whole group may come together and respond interactively, and the mutual discussion and support can be very positive; there can be a real understanding and sharing of feelings among the students and often some follow-up support is informally arranged. One student described the group as her 'life-line.'

Most students, however, prefer to see the tutor–counsellor on their own in the Unit where, as with any counselling service, the room is made relaxing and non-threatening. There are again set hours for this but sometimes their anxieties are so great that they need a point of contact available outside these hours. This may simply involve talking to the tutor over the telephone; indeed one student was guided through the evening before her finals by a series of telephone calls in the course of which she was talked through a panic attack, and offered suggestions on last-minute revision and examination strategy for the following day. A visit to a student's room, however, is very often a shrewd indicator of the type of stress a dyslexic student may suffer: her personal belongings may be in total disarray, there can be piles of washing to be done, she might not be eating properly, her work could be hopelessly disorganised with notes and books scattered untidily around. In short, she has lost control of her own coping strategies and organisation, and her personal welfare and academic welfare are suffering. Under stress a student's problems can seem to him or her quite overwhelming; coupled with this a dyslexic student may not have a very good sense of timing, so the demands upon a tutor–counsellor to offer support at such crisis moments can be quite considerable. It is, of course, to be borne in mind that many dyslexic students have had very supportive parents or teachers and can at times feel isolated at university. Finally, it is important of course to impart to the students that all work of this nature is totally confidential; names are never released without the student's permission.

What has thus evolved from work with the student group is a clear indication of the difficulties facing a dyslexic student at university. This stress will now be examined in more detail, looking first at the particular demands of university life and their effect upon the dyslexic student, second at the more deep-rooted anxieties that may exacerbate the reactions of many students to themselves and their work in this specialised environment, and finally some ways in which we might 'manage' the stress of dyslexic students are discussed.

Specific stress factors in study at undergraduate level

University study operates almost entirely through the written word in a very specialised environment; this can therefore place great pressure upon dyslexic students. Gauntlett (1990) indicates that dyslexic difficulties persist into adult life and increase in magnitude in situations that place great emphasis on written language skills. Although dyslexic students have proved their abilities by being accepted at university in the first place, academically the discipline is more impersonal and more stringent, and certain skills needed which they may not have used at school (Miles and Gilroy, 1995, Chapter 3). Tackling these skills may highlight difficulties which students might have thought they had overcome, or bring to light new difficulties. McLoughlin et al. (1994) writing on counselling adults for study and work has found that a change in personal or working life increases the likelihood of dyslexia coming to light; this has been shown in the Unit at Bangor by the number of mature students who have returned to learning after several years and who come forward for assessment for the first time.

Coping with university life, both academic and personal, places demands upon the student to have some structure in his weekly routine. University study can be much more open-ended than school or college work, and students have more responsibility for their own private study. There seems to be more free time to fill in; there is no set homework timetable and submission dates for essays are often set weeks ahead. This may necessitate organising a study timetable, coping with dead-lines, getting to the library and dealing with books on short loan. This can involve planning and time-management tasks which can be very stressful for a dyslexic student; organising study also places many demands upon the short-term memory – there is usually much diverse information to process during an academic week. Our dyslexic students have often described themselves as having 'cluttered brains'. Stacey (1994) writing as a dyslexic states:

> . . . our minds are wired differently so that we think in unexpected ways . . .
> The result is that we've ended up with muddle in our minds.

This 'muddle' can of course lead to a holistic, lateral, creative way of thinking; however, it can also result in an overcrowding of the brain so that the student cannot sort out the thoughts into clear structures, particularly when stressed. Coupled with this, an analysis of the work patterns of the students in the study group reveals that, in general, dyslexic students have to work longer and harder than their non-dyslexic peer group to achieve the same ends – often written assignments will take twice as long. It is harder for them to catch up by dashing off work quickly; even catching up on a missed lecture may be very difficult because it will be difficult for them to copy out someone else's lecture notes. The awareness of this can at times make students quite bitter. Students may feel that their lecturers do not appreciate the amount of effort they have put into their work – this is often highlighted in labora-tory reports, when dyslexic students have performed very ably in the practical but then get a low mark because of the way they have written the work up.

Certain aspects of study in higher education can cause dyslexic students stress because they place demands on areas in which they have specific difficulties.

McLoughlin et al. (1994) sees the major difficulty for dyslexic adults as being 'an inefficient working memory'. There are also difficulties in processing rapid information and a continuing slowness in reading speed (Miles, 1986).The psychologists' reports on many of our students reveal slower than average reading and writing speeds. As much teaching in higher education is done by formal lectures, note-taking in lectures can therefore prove extremely stressful for a dyslexic student. Many courses are now structured on a modular system – hence there may be up to 200 students in one lecture, a difficult number for a lecturer to cope with, and lectures may be given at speed, supplemented by the use of overhead projectors; thus there is a large amount of information to be processed under fairly stressful conditions and dyslexic students can easily fall behind. This can lead to difficulties with concentration; the processing involved in intense and rapid reading and writing can tire the brain and the eyes, and dyslexic students often find that they can work only for short spaces of time. At university there is usually a heavy reading commitment, with larger more complex textbooks than were used at school; there is probably not the tutor guidance that was perhaps given on 'A' level or BTEC courses and some dyslexic students find it difficult to extract information efficiently from their textbooks. They may also have difficulty in coping with the amount of new, unfamiliar vocabulary. Again lengthy reading tasks can cause considerable tiredness; one student wrote, 'my reading is quite good now but I still find it fatiguing'. Some students may also find themselves faced with having to read aloud; universities are developing 'student-centred' learning where students read tutorial papers or present seminars; this can reawaken the horrors of having to read aloud in class for many students and they find a 'public performance', as one of our students described it, very stressful to cope with in front of a large peer group, many of whom do not know that they are dyslexic.

The difficulties of structuring, organising and timing also occur in writing tasks. Essays at university are lengthier; they need careful planning and referencing, and an objective academic style has to be acquired. Spelling always remains a major difficulty (Gregg, 1983); in fact some students report that spellchecks make them feel more stressed because they highlight the number of mistakes and can also cause further confusion if the student does not know which alternative correct spelling to choose. Tiredness also leads to poor sequencing and structuring in written communication, which manifest themselves in a marked deterioration in spelling, handwriting and computing. At certain points in the term, certain students go through patches of extreme fatigue where they almost come to a standstill – this can happen after examinations or after an intense period of work.

There are certain times in a university career that are particularly stressful for the dyslexic student. The very early days at university can place heavy demands on memory, organisation, orientation. There is the stress of the new environment and the anxiety of coping with new names, relationships, activities and a new lifestyle. (Macfarlane and

McPherson, 1994, describe 'fresher pressure' on non-dyslexics as leading to anxiety, panic and depression.) There is usually a heavy load of introductory forms to fill in and financial arrangements to carry out. Apart from this there are the demands of the new academic disciplines. Dyslexic students may worry intensely about their new pieces of work, wondering whether they have achieved the correct academic standard and struggling with, for example, the new vocabulary they are having to learn. The new students therefore need sympathetic support and consideration during their first weeks at university.

Emotional factors

When starting university, a student may also face a difficult personal decision, which is whether or not he will, in this new environment, admit to his dyslexia. From a sample of 80 students observed at Bangor, 15 have wished to conceal their dyslexia completely. All of these students were diagnosed after the age of 15; perhaps implicit in their wish are bitter memories of school humiliation and fear of 'exposure'. Gauntlett (1990), in a study of dyslexic adults, states that a lack of understanding by many of the people with whom they have come into contact has meant that the 'majority' must continue to conceal their difficulty. Out of these 15 students, four had families who found their child's dyslexia hard to accept, and the students had not been able to discuss their problems at home. Students sometimes state that they have had the dyslexia 'label' firmly attached to them at school and have decided to start again 'incognito' at university; perhaps they now wish to assert more control over their lives and their studies. Others, commendably, wish to make the same start and to move on through the course on equal terms with everyone else. In acute cases not even the friends of these students know that they are dyslexic. This means that they are constantly living with a secret, constantly putting into operation 'avoidance tactics' and constantly worried about the fear of being 'discovered'. This living with concealment must inevitably lead to the build-up of stress whenever a situation occurs in which the dyslexic symptoms are likely to be revealed.

It will be evident therefore that it will be a moment of great anxiety when such a student decides to come forward to seek help because he is now having to admit his failure and break down the barriers he has erected between himself and the world (in fact some of our students talk about 'coming out'). The student is having to ask for help when his very secrecy has indicated that previously he was determined to cope on his own. To him it can be loss of face, humiliation; one student described it as a 'nightmare' that he 'was trapped yet again by dyslexia'. His stress at this initial stage of a relationship with a tutor may manifest itself in off-putting behaviour, aggressiveness and abrasiveness. He may seem rude and abrupt or he may adopt diversionary tactics, partly to prove again what he can do and partly because it is painful to face up to the problems for which he has sought help. One student recently came and apologised for the 3 weeks of aggression he had shown me, but admitted, 'You will never know what it took out of me having to come and see you for the first time'.

Perhaps the most stressful time is the examination and pre-examination period. Peelo (1994, p. 32) writes graphically of the fears of non-dyslexic students facing examinations in words that seem equally applicable to dyslexic students:

> They are frightened of shadows lurking at the back of the brain: I'll let everyone down, I'm stupid, I'm a fraud, this isn't going to work. Which leads to even heavier thoughts: I'll fail, I have no future, I'll be humiliated, I'll have no life.

Hales (1990) shows that among dyslexics those revealing greatest anxiety are those facing the stresses of examinations and career choices. The revision period is difficult because there is no external structure: the student is 'free' to work on his revision in his own time; there are the notes from the year's work to go through, and often they might not make sense. The student is having to work hard on memorising and the memory can become overloaded. Fear of the examination itself can place an inordinate amount of stress on a dyslexic student and, as has already been stated, in some universities students have to fight for their own examination provision. There have been cases of students being charged with being a nuisance by asking for examination provision and of being reminded of the financial implications of their extra invigilation. The actual examination period can again be difficult, because dyslexics find the pressure of writing, working against time and reading carefully very tiring. It is a period when it is important to keep a vigilant eye on a student with special needs. In addition it is not difficult for examination fear to lead to a failing complex. A student who has had prolonged failure in the past may easily expect to continue to fail. Sloboda (1990) noted how anxiety about examinations led to a low expectation of future success in non-dyslexic students and many dyslexic students show little confidence about their future results.

The pressure of academic study can make a dyslexic student very tense and liable to underperform. Raaheim and Wankowski (1981) point out that susceptibility to high emotionality and consequently greater proneness to reactive depression can be regarded as a powerful factor in academic failure. From observations of the behaviour pattern of the students in our study group over a period of time, it is evident that they experience intense high or low reactions to the success or failure of their academic work; they can become easily upset by negative criticism and react very strongly to what they see as 'hostile' or unfair comments on essays. To dyslexics these comments open up old scars. Evans and Smith (1979) evaluated dyslexic clients as being very sensitive to criticism and easily discouraged. Sometimes a student will not hand any work in because she is so anxious about it.

To some extent, however, this type of stress can be self-induced. A dyslexic student may not see that other (non-dyslexic) students have to undergo the acceptance of negative criticism to learn and advance. He may blame everything on dyslexia; we have had several pieces of work sent to us which have been below standard for reasons not necessarily related to dyslexia – poor referencing, irrelevant material, unsubstantiated comment – the student may find it difficult to accept that the marking of these pieces may be justified. This could reflect a state of self-centredness. Dyslexia is ever-present in the students' minds; it makes them egocentric, and they cannot think out from themselves. As a result, they become quite demanding over their 'rights' and may go bluntly into a tutor's room to seek 'justice'. In turn the tutor grows more hostile and the stress builds up on both sides. With some dyslexic people this can be linked to a lack of self-awareness – 'we lack the perception of things' (Hargrave Wright, 1994) – which is particularly noticeable when students are under stress.

Many other students exhibit a strong streak of perfectionism which in itself is very stressful; they seem to want to overprove themselves. An obsessive working pattern with impossibly high standards can result; one student asked me to help her improve on her folder of essays – there were in fact three A's and two B's. Another student drove himself too hard in the pre-examination period, worked for extremely long hours and in fact ended up with a much lower class of degree than he should have had. This, again, can happen to any student but a dyslexic student has a high anxiety factor and it is harder for him or her to put a clarifying structure on an overloaded brain.

Students also experience the good days and bad days, as recounted by Susan Hampshire (1981) and Eileen Simpson (1981). Stacey (1994) also refers to the good/bad day syndrome. 'Bad days' affect the students in various ways, often making them frustrated because their difficulties seem stronger and get in the way of their academic progress. There are days when they cannot use the dictionary or take notes, when they cannot work out the library coding system, when they misread timetables and go to the wrong room. These 'bad days' can be stressful for dyslexic students, because it can make them feel 'different' from their non-dyslexic friends. 'Bad days' may be linked to tiredness which can be a source of anxiety for students as they realise that they cannot work for long periods in comparison to their peers – students have, for example, reported feeling acute tiredness and subsequent stress in 2-hour group teaching sessions in the Computer Laboratory and felt that they coped far less well than their non-dyslexic peers. Jean Augur (1985) in 'Guidelines for teachers, parents and learners' lists 21 key points of being dyslexic, one of which is 'excessive tiredness due to the amount of concentration and effort required', but many of our students find this difficult to come to terms with.

Anxiety and panic

Highly anxious students are prone to panic which represents another form of acute stress. The student may panic when faced with tasks in which his dyslexia may be exposed – virtually every student dreads writing cheques. Michael Vinegrad working on a checklist for detecting dyslexic adults found, for example, that writing cheques was the most common and positive indicator (Vinegrad, 1994). Students report feeling panic under rapid-processing tasks such as note-taking and, of course, examinations. Once panic sets in, the mind might seize up and the student can do very little. Most students report having experienced moments during examinations when their minds go blank; they have described them as being 'like cotton wool', 'like falling into a muddy puddle', 'like being nailed to the floor'.

An extension to this type of panic-related stress occurs when the symptoms of blankness can go on for a period of time; the student's coping strategy is, in fact, not to cope but to opt out and she can come to a complete standstill. In cases observed, it seems that there has been an accumulation of work with which she cannot cope, maybe a series of deadlines that she cannot achieve. The sequencing tasks involved in sorting out what she has to do are too complex and the student can neither structure nor see a clear pattern so that even the simplest tasks become immense. Personal communication even becomes a burden. Several students have gone through lengthy periods of inertia and inactivity. One student this year started to sleep heavily and it seemed that the lengthy hours, resulting at first from extreme tiredness, became a means of escaping from the round of tutorials and lectures that he had missed and which had then become too onerous for him to catch up with. At its most extreme one student negotiated for a complete year off; he needed a total change and relaxation of his system and in fact got a very good degree after returning to university for his final year. This type of stress may be difficult for the tutor or counsellor to deal with because the student may not have the physical or mental energy or indeed the necessary organisational skills to come and seek help. It is at this stage that a counsellor may have to take a more assertive role and visit the student at home, or find out what has happened through one of his friends. The counsellor will of course have to weigh up the situation: the student may not be ready to receive help and may wish to be left on his own. In some cases, however, a student seems unable to be guided into any decisions and wants the counsellor to assume a more directive role.

This may involve helping the student to prioritise, perhaps by creating an 'action list', such as a highly structured timetable starting with very short sessions. Students suffering this pattern of stress need careful monitoring.

Acute anxiety shows itself in another, indeed opposite, form, when the student reacts to his difficulties by becoming overactive; his mind becomes confused and he seems unable to structure or unscramble his thoughts: Mueller (1979) discussed the interference of anxiety with the cognitive capacity to study; dyslexic students can dart from topic to topic in conversation and make illogical jumps in essay writing. Their work gets disorganised and the pattern of stress becomes self-perpetuating. They create disorder around themselves and can see no way out; therefore the disorder in their minds gets worse. Their stress may be reflected in their physical appearance, their eye movements and their body language. It is again important to help the student gain a structure in his work, perhaps even work with him on the details of his day-to-day life pattern.

Personal relationships

Some dyslexic students can be quite withdrawn and solitary. Hales (1990, 1994) in his work on personality factors in dyslexic people has found that certain groups of dyslexic adolescents prefer to work on their own, have fewer friends and find it difficult to join in with others. These traits have been shown by some students in the group, particularly when they are under stress; they become quite isolated, in which case their anxieties become intensified because they may not find people with whom they can discuss their difficulties. For other reasons too a dyslexic student may suffer a sense of isolation. His general dyslexic problems may have led to tensions within the family and to his own feeling of separateness at school. As has already been pointed out, a dyslexic student generally has to work much harder than a non-dyslexic student and this again cuts him off from some of the socialising so necessary to student life. This can lead to a sense of envy of others; many a student has used the phrase 'it's not fair'. They may be aware that other students do not have to work as hard as they do, or can seem to dash off an essay in one overnight session and still get good marks. This can lead to a begrudging or even bitter attitude which can make for difficulty in personal relationships.

Over the years I have worked with dyslexic students I have also noticed a high incidence of illness: two students have had myalgic encephalomyelitis (ME); two have had irritable bowel syndrome; many suffer from skin trouble; and many seem to have recurring throat problems. These seem to be related to stress. Another indication of anxiety is eating problems which seem to occur fairly regularly; these can be exacerbated by dyslexia, because when a dyslexic is under stress a visit to a shop or supermarket can be quite a daunting experience. One student lived off bananas and milk because it did not make any demands on her. Two students have developed a stammer under stress.

The point needs to be reinforced that these students are away from any support structures that they may have had at school or home, and perhaps from a familiar environment where their dyslexia was known and understood. They may have been considered high fliers at school and then may find themselves in a situation where their dyslexic difficulties are brought out more intensely. Although the climate of opinion towards dyslexia is changing in universities, there are still members of staff who are not sympathetic and who see dyslexics as failing to conform to their rigorous academic standards or to the traditional methods of examination. Unless there is a dyslexia support tutor, the student often has to fight his own battles, seeing staff about his difficulties and asking for his own provisions. She or he may undergo a wearisome search through the university, looking for support; we receive many telephone calls and letters in the Unit, where students are appealing for sources of help. I can quote from one such letter:

> ... fends find it difficult to beie [believe] that I don't get A for exams as I really unperstand the metarial given. My letres [lecturers] do not unrerstand the problem, and so I wondrer if you had any material to which I could gie them.

Seeking such help can be very time-consuming and is often seen by the student as quite a humiliating experience.

Apart from this, the student is usually living an independent life. This again demands organisation and time management and makes many demands on short-term memory. The student has to cope with his own personal communication – we have had examples of students not being able to fill in passport forms or to write coherent business letters. Dyslexic students can now claim the Disabled Students' Allowance and the procedures for this can cause them a considerable amount of worry – the Unit in fact issues the students with a step-by-step guide to this process and yet many students delay in claiming their allowance simply because they cannot face the paperwork involved. There are also the many money problems faced by the modern generation of students, which entail visits to the bank, dealing with credit cards, applying for access funds. Most students face career guidance in their third year at college but for dyslexics this can be quite a stressful activity because applying for jobs involves letter writing and creating a curriculum vitae, apart from filling in application forms and attending interviews – all this at the time of working for finals.

The effect of past experiences on self-concept

It can therefore be seen that the particular nature of dyslexia coupled with the stringent disciplines of university life can cause students considerable anxiety with their academic work. There is, however, a much deeper psychological perspective to the stress patterns of many dyslexic students. There are certain students with more deep-rooted insecurities which stem from the past, from having been branded as 'thick', from being ridiculed and misunderstood, from having struggled hard at school without efforts being recognised. These insecurities may be latent: they create a tentative, underconfident attitude to work; they can re-emerge forcefully when the student feels that she is losing control of her work or when she has received negative comment. It therefore becomes very evident that the emotional stress suffered in childhood or adolescence has had a very deep-rooted effect. Kline (1978) spoke of the 'emotional carnage' of adolescents with dyslexia in a paper which preceded 'Robin's story' (Jones, 1978), a mother's account of her dyslexic son who committed suicide. Rawson (1988) refers to the 'scars' (p. 47) left by dyslexia and Stevens (1987) describes the acute underconfidence of the learning-disabled adolescent. Miles (1993) states that most dyslexic children whom he has met have faced appreciable hardship. Many of our students have written about their school experiences:

> While I was at school I was educated to feel shame and worthlessness, to feel doubt in my own abilities and self-hatred. I was educated to feel small and useless.

> During this time my mother was told X is educationally subnormal and will never gain any examination grades.

> There was a terror campaign waged against me to get me to spell properly.

And from a poem:

> A hundred childehood years
> I stumbeld thruoh
> clutching at gors yelow flowrs
> that promised sunliet
> in this boalder-gray clif-egde
> of wrieting.

It is obvious that past experiences leave a deep scar and that many dyslexic students have a poor self-concept and suffer from low self-esteem. This was shown by Griffiths (1975) who noted that a group of dyslexic students saw themselves as less intelligent than their peers. The students I have worked with quite often compare themselves unfavourably with their peer group. In listening to a spontaneous, undirected, general conversation lasting about 20 minutes between five students, the following words and phrases were noted: 'hopeless at' (seven times); 'useless at' (five times); 'could never' (three times); 'mess' (twice); 'typical me' (twice); 'never been any good at' . The use of 'never' and 'typical' indicate that the poor self-image stretches back to child-hood and is therefore quite deep rooted. In answer to a specifically directed question following this conversation four out of the five students said that they often felt that they were 'thick'. We can think of Margaret Rawson's description of 'Dyslexia Day in Community Park': there are many individuals present:

> . . . yet perhaps more often than is really comfortable we sense psychological stress, worry, and, in some cases almost palpable discouragement.

Rawson (1988, p. 21)

This is borne out by an interesting perspective which has emerged in the Bangor student group over the last few years; since 1990 the number of mature students in the study group has increased by 60 per cent. Some of these mature students are new assessees, some have been out of education because of their dyslexic difficulties and have re-entered, perhaps through Access courses. Many of these students have lived with their difficulties in the past, suffered from them, but not become aware of them until university and then had to face up to them – yet they entered university with high expectations. For a mature student to be newly assessed as dyslexic can be very stressful; old fears and negative thoughts well up from the past, there is often anger at past neglect, there are worries about being 'disabled', about implications for children, for careers. These students can be extremely underconfident and hence very anxious; they can also get very frustrated. They contrast with a newly emerging group of 18 year olds who have benefited from the 1981 Education Act, been assessed at a young age and who have grown up with the knowledge that they are dyslexic. To a large extent they have learnt to come to terms with it and have also developed a more positive attitude. They seek help with their studies but do not suffer the deep-rooted anxieties of these other students.

Developing coping strategies

It is therefore evident that the particular stringencies of university life would suggest that it is advantageous for dyslexic students to have some specialist support. The overall aim of this support should be to alleviate the student's stress by getting him to understand his particular way of working, and hence helping him to feel that he can control his learning metacognitively so that he will approach it with greater confidence. It is important too that he is aware of his particular areas of difficulty. It is very useful to start with a discussion of dyslexia, which can emphasise the research into the right brain and indicate that dyslexia is constitu-tional in origin (e.g. Galaburda et al., 1989) – it is surprising how few students really know very much about what dyslexia is – and look at the positive ways in which a dyslexic student can use his particular skills to learn (West, 1991, appeals particularly to the students). The student should of course be made aware of multisensory techniques for every aspect of his learning. The study skills teaching should emphasise planning and organisation, and help the student to find his or her way of coping with time management and memory and concentration. All students benefit from help with note-taking, both from books and lectures, and various ways of taking notes can be practised. Mind mapping (Buzan, 1974) is particularly useful. Good notes can teach planning and structure and hence lead on to the teaching of essay writing. Into this can be incorporated ongoing spelling and language tuition for these are often the biggest worries of dyslexic students. Virtually all dyslexic students are now computer literate and there are many new technological aids such as Voice-type talking programs and scanners (Hutchins, 1994) which can be of immense benefit in relieving the student's worries about writing and editing. Dyslexic students need particular help and care during the revision and examination period, where discussion on memory, multisensory learning and work organisation can be initiated, the aim of the tutor being to help the student to work efficiently on his own and to prevent him from becoming tired, strained, disorganised. Given this type of study support many students can come to terms with their stress. Stacey (1994, p. 12) in her article for other dyslexics says 'The good news is that you can learn what you want to when you find the right teacher'.

The role of the counsellor

Into this study skills work will inevitably be entwined a strong element of personal counselling. Ideally counselling work with dyslexic students would be based on the general theories formulated by Carl Rogers (1951), in which counselling is seen as a 'client-based enterprise' where the student is led to discover his own process and techniques of learning. However, dyslexia is a specific condition which is inextricably bound up with the student's anxieties; it seems that at times the counselling process may need to move towards being directive, that is, the counsellor becomes a teacher, even an organiser, and provides specific help and advice with the very problems that are causing the student confusion and uncertainty. In *Student Counselling in Practice*, Newsome et al. (1973) describe this more specific type of counselling skill as 'the ability to match the impression that we are building up of the person and his problem against those which constitute well-defined clinical or sub-clinical syndromes' (p. 47). Counselling in dyslexia has been discussed more specifically by Miles (1988) who distinguishes between 'generalist' and 'specialist' counselling, and a more structured approach for general student study skills has also been discussed by Sieber et al. (1977), who state that highly anxious students particularly benefit from methods that provide a high degree of structure and organisation so that they can make up for their own deficiencies in structuring material.

The counsellor therefore needs to listen with care and empathy to the student's anxieties. There will be decisions to make about how to work with him and how to balance language therapy with restoring the student's self-confidence and battered self-image. As has already been discussed, when a dyslexic student comes to seek help he may be in a state of great anxiety. He may have had endless years of remedial work at school and have thought that he had overcome his problems. If he then receives bad marks at university, he may feel a failure yet again, exposed, vulnerable, inadequate. If he brings a page of error-ridden spellings, or an essay that has been criticised for poor structure, he may desperately need to have help to sort them out and it will be important for the tutor to do what will offer the most immediate relief to the student. Kline and Kline (1973) cite cases where beginning with language therapy rather than psychotherapy alleviates the stress or reduces the anxiety to a controlled proportion. There are, however, students who cannot face any language work; their morale has been shattered by getting bad marks and they feel out of control. Sometimes they may feel angry and frustrated that their knowledge is not coming out in the way they want it to; someone beginning to teach them more spelling and grammar may make them feel more threatened and even more exposed and out of control.

For these students it is more important to listen to their difficulties and their past insecurities. Many of the students who have used the Unit have said that they have experienced a great sense of relief that at last they can have a meaningful discussion about the problems of being dyslexic. About one-third of the students have said that they have found real understanding of their problems only for the first time at this level, and that this is the first time that they have spoken openly with someone outside their immediate family. This means that they have had years of school or adult life during which they have been unable to vent their feelings and hence have become accustomed to bottling up their anger and frustration. The 'specialist' approach to counselling is integral to the whole process, because it is the communication of an understanding of what dyslexia is and the effects it has that will create the most meaningful relationship between counsellor and student. Many of the subjects we have worked with at Bangor have said that having someone to understand their anxieties and frustrations was very important. Over two evenings six university students in the group blamed on stress simple errors such as inability to recall the alphabet, inability to do simple maths, simple mistakes made on the computer. The students were aware of their difficulties and felt that it can be very embarrassing to talk about such 'mistakes' to people who do not understand. Miles (1993) states, from his experience, that many dyslexics need constant reassurance that they are not 'thick' or stupid. Dyslexic undergraduates have a lurking fear that they are not bright enough to be at university; this fear can become dominant when the student starts to feel anxious about his work. Part of stress management therefore should be to help the student to see himself in a more positive light; one student was recently encouraged by looking at the degree results of recent graduates – he needed that reassurance; role-models of successful dyslexic people are also encouraging.

A further aspect of a more directive way of dealing with the student's stress is to discuss with him how far his difficulties should be communicated to those who encounter him during the academic term. Some tutors do not understand how difficult it is for students to, for example, read aloud in class, or to take tests or orals. They may not have any sympathy for constantly late essay submissions or understand the sensitivity a dyslexic student might feel. A counsellor can intervene on the student's behalf and hence preclude any further fear of his being put in a stressful situation.

When I first meet dyslexic students I chat to them about being dyslexic and at some stage I indicate to them that they might find themselves prone to stress; I feel that with this awareness they themselves can be more prepared for it and perhaps more able to cope with it. We often discuss coping strategies. I have implied the value of group work; it can be very positive for dyslexic students to come together as a group and share their feelings. They begin to realise that they are not alone, that their difficulties are experienced by others and that they can discuss mutual ways of coping. Discussion, for example, about their varying memory techniques, can be very useful. So, too, can a shared sense of humour – they can tell each other the funny things that they have done, whereas they could not laugh at themselves to 'outsiders'. It is interesting to read in Hicks (1990) that, in a study of dyslexic schoolchildren, they said that the quality they admired most in a teacher was 'a sense of humour'.

Relaxation therapies

I encourage the students to practise progressive relaxation; yoga is very useful – it helps to concentrate the mind. We practise deep breathing and practise 'slowing down' – stopping what one is doing and clearing the mind before coping with one immediate task. We have tried juggling. Some of our students have used aromatherapy; some have practised reflexology; all of them listen to music – one student said it created 'a safe sort of little world'. We discuss creative visualisation (Shone, 1984). I emphasise the importance of fresh air and exercise (preferably simple, non-competitive exercise such as swimming) and when I see a stressed student I almost always ask if he or she is eating properly. We discuss lists and prioritisation, the aim being to get the student to take things one step at a time and not to let his mind 'kangaroo' as one student described his overactive brain. Several of our students have developed creative hobbies, such as pottery or photography or drawing, which give them a real sense of escape – and achievement.

In conclusion, it would be useful if every teacher and tutor working with dyslexic students realised the importance of helping these students to maintain a positive self-concept and looked carefully at the links between language therapy and personal support. With greater inner confidence a student might be able to overcome the stress and anxiety that can become quite inhibiting to his academic progress. It has been sadly illuminating to realise the effect of early struggles and difficulties upon many dyslexic undergraduates and to see how deep-rooted their underconfidence has become, and also how much determination and strength it takes for these undergraduates to cope with university discipline. Personal counselling aimed at supporting the dyslexic student as a 'whole person' should ideally be part of every study skills programme at every level of education.

References

Augur J (1985). Guidelines for teachers, parents and learners. In M Snowling (Ed.), *Children's Written Language Difficulties*. London: NFER-Nelson.

Buzan T (1974). *Use Your Head*. London: BBC.

Evans JR, Smith LJ (1979). Common behavioral SLD characteristics. *Academic Therapy* XII(4): 425–9.

Galaburda AM, Rosen GF, Sherman G. (1989). The neural origin of developmental dyslexia. In AM Galaburda (Ed.), *From Reading to Neurons*. Cambridge, MA: MIT Press.

Gauntlett D (1990). Managing the dyslexic adult. In G Hales, M Hales, T Miles, A Summerfield (Eds), *Meeting Points in Dyslexia*, pp. 240–4. Reading: British Dyslexia Association.

Gilroy DE (1991). *Dyslexia and Higher Education*. Bangor: University of Wales Dyslexia Unit.

Gregg N (1983). College learning disabled writer. *Journal of Learning Disabilities* 16: 334–8.

Griffiths AN (1975). Self-concepts of dyslexic children. *Academic Therapy* 11: 83–90.

Hales G (Ed.) (1990). Personality aspects of dyslexia. In *Meeting Points in Dyslexia*, pp. 98–103. Reading: BDA.

Hales G (Ed.) (1994). The human aspects of dyslexia. In *Dyslexia Matters*, pp. 172–83. London: Whurr.

Hampshire S (1981). *Susan's Story*. London: Sidgwick & Jackson.

Hargrave Wright J (1994). Coping strategies for adult dyslexics. *Dyslexia Contact* 13(2): 6–7.

Hicks C (1990). Dyslexic, retarded and normal reader's perceptions of the qualities of real and ideal class teachers. *British Educational Research Journal* 16: 199–207.

Hutchins J (1994). How computers can help the dyslexic adult. *Dyslexia Contact* **13**(1): 20–1.

Jones FE (1978). Robin's story. *Bulletin of the Orton Society* **XXVIII**: 175–81.

Kline CL (1978). Developmental dyslexia in adolescence: the emotional carnage. *Bulletin of the Orton Society* **XXVIII**: 160–75.

Kline CL, Kline CL (1973). Severe reading disabilities: the family's dilemma. *Bulletin of the Orton Society* **XXIII**: 146–60.

Macfarlane A, McPherson A (1994). *Fresher Pressure: How to Survive as a Student*. Oxford: Oxford Paperbacks.

McLoughlin D, Fitzgibbon G, Young V (1994). *Adult Dyslexia: Assessment, Counselling and Training*. London: Whurr.

Miles TR (1986). On the persistence of dyslexic difficulties into adulthood. In GTh Pavlidis, DF Fisher (Eds), *Dyslexia: Its Neuropsychology and Treatment*. Chichester: Wiley.

Miles TR (1988). Counselling in dyslexia. *Counselling Psychology Quarterly* **I**: 97–107.

Miles TR (1993). *Understanding Dyslexia*. Bath: Amethyst Books.

Miles TR, Gilroy DE (1995). *Dyslexia at College*, 2nd edn. London: Routledge.

Milner P (1980). *Counselling in Education*. London: Dent.

Mueller JH (1979). Test anxiety and the encoding and retrieval of information. In IG Sarason (Ed.), *Test Anxiety: Theory, Research and Application*. Hillsdale: Laurence Erlbaum Associates.

Newsome A, Thorne BJ, Wyld K (1973). *Student Counselling in Practice*. London: University of London.

Peelo M (1994). *Helping Students with Study Problems*. Buckingham: SRHE & OU.

Raaheim K, Wankowski J (1981). *Helping Students to Learn at University*. Bergen: Sigma Forlag.

Rawson MB (1988). *The Many Faces of Dyslexia*. Baltimore, MD: Orton Dyslexia Society.

Rogers C (1951). *Client-centered Therapy*. Boston: Houghlin Mifflin.

Shone R (1984). *Creative Visualization*. London: Aquarian/Thorsons.

Siebler JE, O'Neil HF, Tobias S (1977). *Anxiety, Learning and Instruction*. Hillsdale: Laurence Erlbaum Associates.

Simpson E (1981). *Reversals*. London: Gollancz.

Sloboda J (1990). Combating examination stress among university students. *British Journal of Guidance and Counselling* **18**: 124–36.

Stacey G (1994). Dyslexia from the inside. *Dyslexia Contact* **15**(1): 12–13.

Stevens R (1987). The learning disabled adolescent. *SPELD*: 3–6.

Vinegrad M (1994). A revised Adult Dyslexia Check List. *Educare* **48**: 21–4.

West T (1991). *In the Mind's Eye*. Buffalo, NY: Prometheus.

Chapter 6
Stress factors in the work-place

GERALD HALES

'Hello, this is Smith Engineering. Can I help you?'
'I'm enquiring about the job in today's paper.'
'Oh yes. We're taking names and sending out information. Where do you live?'
'Harmondswyke.'
'Can you spell that please?'. . . .

'Hello, this is Smith Engineering. Can I help you?'
'I'm enquiring about the job in today's paper.'
'Oh yes. We're taking names and sending out information. You have to complete the forms and send them back by next Monday.'
'Thank you.'. . . .

'Hello, this is Smith Engineering. Can I help you?'
'I'm enquiring about the job in today's paper.'
'Oh yes. You have to send in a letter of application.'. . . .

'Hello, this is Smith Engineering. Can I help you?'
'I'm enquiring about the job in today's paper.'
'Oh yes. You have to contact Mr Joplin-Smythe at Head Office I'll-give-you-the address-it's-Dearing-and-Cross-Engineering-Limited-Dearing-House-34-Crescent-Street-Bristol-BS43-8QZ-Have-you-got-all-that?.'. . .

It is the experience of many dyslexic people that being dyslexic creates stress in the workplace. However, any attempt to collect statistics or numbers would almost certainly under-estimate the extent of the difficulty because many dyslexic people find that the barriers arise before they can manage to reach the workplace. The scenarios above do not represent anything unreasonable or out of the ordinary on the part of the company. The procedures suggested are not in any sense strange or uncommon. It is for this reason that they tend to create even more stress among dyslexic people, first because they meet such situations frequently, and second because they know that their difficulty arises in circumstances that are not considered strange or difficult. It is not difficult to become frustrated and depressed under those conditions.

Stress is not any sort of inadequacy in the individual or just a temporary reaction to an inability to cope. The reactions to stressful situations are physical as well as emotional and psychological, and continued experience of stress can lead to such problems as high blood pressure and heart disease. An endocrinologist who has carried out major research into the effects of stress upon the body makes it clear that if a stress response is chronic, the constant presence of stress hormones begins to wear down the body's immunological system; whatever part of the body is weakest will show signs of dysfunction first (Selye, 1978).

It is not possible to separate entirely the stress arising from dyslexia at work and the day-to-day problems that are produced. Although this chapter – and this book – addresses primarily the stress aspect, this is inextricably linked to the practical situations with which dyslexic people have to cope. In spite of the common perception that both dyslexia and stress are factors that have only recently become 'popular', we have known for many years that the interaction of these has been a source of a great deal of difficulty in many people's lives (Witty, 1950; Beare, 1975). Not only has this included the aspect of stress and stress reactions, but also lower levels of self-esteem, and a more restricted level of work and vocational opportunities; it will surprise few readers that this often means that the dyslexic worker's economic situation is not always as good as might otherwise have been expected. The following are the main steps in which the stress aspect is likely to come to the fore:

- Applying for a job
- Interviews
- The first day(s)
- Coping with the job (or coping with trying to hide the problem!)
- Promotion.

This discussion of the work environment will follow this pattern.

Before you even have a job

Almost all jobs, whether large or small, full-time or part-time, important or trivial, require the completion of an application form. Some dyslexic people find this task so daunting that they do not manage to progress beyond the stage of looking at the form! Why is it a problem?

The reasons stem back to the general underlying difficulties experienced by the dyslexic person. Although it has often true that the major symptoms are seen in areas such as reading, writing and spelling, the problems that arise when doing these tasks are in reality only the external symptoms of what is happening in the brain. Put in its most general form, the problems are those of organisation, especially of sequencing. An application form has an organisational structure – quite probably a very rigid one – but the chances of it matching the way dyslexic individuals organise the way that they think are very small! To complete a form, the dyslexic person must try to fit his knowledge into the strait-jacket of someone else's structure, and this is very difficult. At best it raises the level of stress; at worst it is cast aside and never done.

We must also not lose sight of the fact that even where the form is completed it takes a long time to do. Time is a major aspect of most dyslexic people's lives, and performance is frequently a constant trade-off between speed and accuracy. This means that to do things accurately they take a long time. For an application the applicant needs time for two reasons:

1. To conceptualise each entry in a manner that suits the form.
2. To ensure that items are being entered accurately.

There is an additional aspect that will affect many dyslexic people; this is the fact that forms need to be filled in with a pen. It is now recognised that quite a large percentage of dyslexic people do not always work best with a pen, and the advent of the personal computer and word-processing has made this even more widespread than it used to be. You can't put an application form in the printer, however, unless you intend to go to enormous lengths to format your responses to fit the pre-printed page, and so you are immediately debarred from the method that would create the best impression.

After all, this is one of the major functions of application forms: creating an impression. Although many would deny that this is the primary intention, and that they are meant to convey data about education, experience, skills and knowledge, in reality the overall impression given by an application form is frequently a significant component at the time of short-listing. From the applicant's point of view, an application form has only one purpose – to get you an interview!

What can be done about this? One extremely helpful step would be for employers to be more flexible, more prepared to accept application in different formats. A willingness to accept the same information, but printed out from the applicant's own word-processor, or to consider a general letter of application rather than the specific structure of the form, would alleviate the stress felt by many would-be workers. Of course application forms request specific information, some of which is vital, but in cases where important parts were missing it is not difficult to follow them up, either during interview or separately. If it is really important that the layout and structure of the form be followed, it would not be too difficult in this high-tech age for employers to supply application forms on disk, so that applicants who wished could fill them in on the computer, but as with the introduction of portable computers in schools, there is frequently a lot of resistance to something seen as 'awkward'.

However, it has to be said that employers often lose potentially good employees because the first step in the process tests their writing and form-filling skills. Yet this is (at this stage, at least) not what is wanted. The employer needs to know about the individual – skills, experience, talents, etc. – and this could be just as easily encompassed within a telephone call, perhaps with a preliminary face-to-face discussion.

Reality dictates, however, that it is usually the dyslexic person who must cope with the procedure, and the chances of having the procedure changed much are extremely limited. There are some options to consider, however: in the first place, it is always helpful to take a photocopy of the form (maybe several) so that the task of completing it can be tried out before producing the final version. It is often useful to enlist the assistance of a friend or colleague, and it is quite possible for the writing on the final form to be his or hers! Where there is no choice but to complete it by hand, dyslexic people should consider whether they find such writing easier in capitals or lower-case letters and stick to one or the other.

Interviews: gateway or barrier?

Interviews create stress and anxiety in almost everyone, so in this respect dyslexic people are not alone. Generally speaking, too, it could easily be considered that the oral, verbal context of the interview situation would be better for dyslexic people than other methods. However, there are two aspects which mean that this is not always true:

1. Some dyslexic people have verbal and speech confusions.
2. Some positions will require participation in psychometric testing.

Verbal dyslexia

Dyslexia is often conceived of as a difficulty with areas such as reading, writing and spelling. This is generally perfectly true, but it is easy to forget, and a potential employer may never have known, that these are only the outward symptoms of an organisational inefficiency in the brain itself. In some people, these functional differences also affect speech and verbal output, and so there are those who have difficulty in the oral situation.

We must add to this the effects that stressful experiences have on all of us. When suffering from stress it is more difficult to do things such as carry out detailed tasks requiring high levels of accuracy, be precise over controlling behaviour or be sure that we give precisely the impression of ourselves that we wish. One of the greatest difficulties faced by the dyslexic individual in this sort of circumstance is that a small number of relatively minor errors will increase the level of distress, thereby increasing the likelihood that errors will be made. In this way the procedure becomes something of a self-fulfilling prophecy, as illustrated in Figure 6.1.

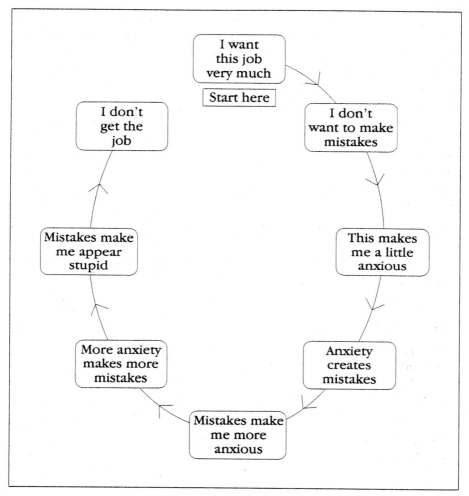

Figure 6.1. The stress conundrum.

Psychometric testing

Psychological evaluations are increasingly being used in the selection process for jobs that have levels of responsibility. In the normal run of events they should not present any applicant with worries beyond the normal anxiety likely to exist about the whole process. They are standardised instruments designed to measure certain aspects of human functioning in an efficient and validated manner. However, for the dyslexic applicant they can raise a number of difficulties.

In the first place many aspects, such as personality questionnaires, are usually of a multiple-choice format, which means that they involve filling in forms again, with the same problems as raised by the application form. Other types, such as Verbal Reasoning tests, are also commonly used to form some estimate of the individual intellectual potential. On a practical level, if the response sheet is designed to be read by a computer, the printing on it may well be in quite faint colours, and this can make it less clear for the dyslexic applicant to see which answers go where (to say nothing of the effect it might have on some colour-blind people). However, there is a point here for the professionals, too. In many dyslexic people their pattern of functioning means that they will not produce scores on a Verbal Reasoning test that do justice to their true intellectual position or potential. It is recommended that for people with this type of difficulty a non-verbal test should be used. However, the stress position can be encountered either way, because if dyslexic people do not say that there is problem they will be faced with a difficult and inappropriate test situation, whereas if they do make a declaration they have the anxieties arising from doing that. The worry then is that they are seen to be awkward, that they ask for 'special treatment', that they give the tester difficulties because non-verbal materials may not be available, and that such matters might result in them being less likely to succeed in the process.

Finally, it must be remembered that interviews require instant responses. The individual is expected to provide reactions, explanations and opinions immediately, but in many areas of life dyslexic people need to take a little time to consider the data and formulate a response that truly reflects their understanding. Often a slow reaction in interview is taken not as a sign of deep thought about the matter in hand, but as an indication that the individual cannot cope as well as others. This is often inaccurate and generally unfair, and the dyslexic candidate knows that, of course; but that knowledge does nothing to reduce the level of stress either!

Taking up the offer: challenge or opportunity?

Many people might be forgiven for thinking that if the individual manages to get through all this and be offered the job all the stress will disappear in a cloud of euphoric relief, and so it almost always does – temporarily. However, the day comes when a new job must be started.

Taking up a new position is stressful for us all. There are new things to learn, new procedures to adopt, new people with whom to establish relationships and a new culture of day-to-day work. The dyslexic person, though, has the following added factors:

1. Coping with all this and the dyslexic mode of operation as well.
2. Stress arising from either telling or not telling people about the dyslexia.

Dyslexia is at its worst when the individual is in 'learning mode'. As the difficulty is one of organising, remembering and utilising information in the right manner, time to consolidate and work through the information learned is very important. This means that situations where more and more information is fed into the system are the hardest of all, and this is exactly what happens (to us all) during the first few days in a new job. It is also why the situation of education or training is frequently particularly hard.

There are many things to 'take in'. This is fairly obvious when we are talking about such elements as company procedures, specific demands of the job, how equipment works, and so on; but it is also true in less obvious ways, such as remembering everyone's name, getting used to a new timetable of the day's work and even finding out how to use a telephone system or input the code for the photocopier! Often it is the unwritten procedures that are more crucial to day-to-day harmony than the official rules. Knowing that Albert always sits in *that* chair, or that only Millicent does *his* typing, are the stuff of which smooth running is made, but are totally non-obvious to the newcomer. Although all newcomers will be forgiven once (or maybe twice) for getting it wrong or forgetting the details, the new dyslexic employee may find it especially difficult to internalise these aspects of life which are not, after all, clear and obvious, and the tolerance of others for apparently stupid lapses will not last long.

It is in this context that the decision will have to be made as to whether to tell people about the dyslexia. It is clear that in an ideal world making the difficulty clear is a good idea. Not only will employers and colleagues not be able to make allowances for it if they do not know about it, but if they are kept in the dark they are not available when the dyslexic individual needs help, assistance or advice. However, there is much evidence that this ideal world is not the world in which most of us live and work, and it is understandable – if regrettable – that some dyslexic people decide that it is wiser to keep their own counsel. It does, of course, increase the stress factor once again, as the new employee is placed in the position of not only having to cope with the difficulties of learning the new job, but also having to do it as a dyslexic person, and additionally working things so that that fact is hidden from everyone! This is a substantial mental juggling act and can easily lead to anxiety levels far in excess of what would otherwise be expected.

We should not underestimate the emotional reactions in this situation. Change is stressful and frightening for us all, but the level may be much greater for the dyslexic person. There may be real fear: fear of failure, fear of ridicule or fear of exposure as 'inadequate' in some way. It may well take the new dyslexic employee much longer than everyone else to internalise the fine points and become fully part of the team.

Doing the job

All the factors mentioned so far are temporary; they are hurdles that it is necessary to climb over, but once over them the individual does land on the other side. Having landed, though, there is then a long-term situation to be faced – that of actually doing the job, hopefully with as much success as everyone else.

The fact that the individual has managed to pass through the selection procedures, survived the interview and settled in to a new position does not mean that the task is over or the difficulties solved. Here we should separate the practical aspects of the person's working practices and the aspects that relate to the person him- or herself. The dyslexic worker is not a deficient piece of office equipment that takes a time to get going, but once it is properly installed all the problems go away. He is a person, with all the reactions, idiosyncrasies and personal perceptions that this implies. We see this, among other things, in the attempts made to compensate for the situations in which the individuals find themselves. Gauntlett (1990) reports that:

> Language learning difficulties were found to have been an interactive influence on the development of the individual's personality. Highly significant differences were found indicating that the dyslexic adult is intelligent but retains an open mind when problem solving and as a lateral thinker is capable of producing unorthodox results.

In the results of research into the personality structures of dyslexic people carried out by me a very high score was found on a measure of dominance, something that increases steadily from childhood (Figure 6.2). The pattern found among the dyslexic adults in that study indicates that they are independent-minded and assertive but also solemn, unconventional and rebellious. In the report of that work it was suggested that this is not surprising, because they need a level of assertiveness – perhaps even stubbornness – to cope with the difficulties they find in life (Hales, 1994).

It is largely recognised now that the dyslexic pupil or student needs specific strategies to be able to pass through education; in the same way the dyslexic adult needs strategies to cope with working life – although this is not yet so commonly recognised. Many of the strategies that could be interpreted as 'work skills' are often an extension of 'life skills', because the differing parts of the dyslexic person's life interact just as they do for everyone else.

This is important in terms of the wider question of 'coping', because it is not only the dyslexic person who has to 'cope', but those who work with him as well. Indeed, this can sometimes be the most major factor; people with all types of disability often say that their real disability is other people and their attitudes, and in this respect dyslexic people are

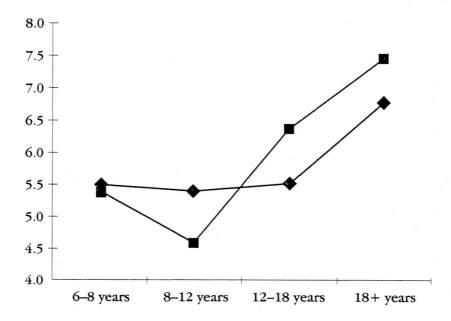

Figure 6.2. Dominance. ──◆── Male, ──■── Female.

no different. Co-workers and superiors will frequently exhibit the common misconception that dyslexic-type errors indicate a low level of competence or intelligence, and the constant worry that they might be 'caught out' by someone with entrenched (erroneous) ideas about the problem is a source of high anxiety levels for many. Even when matters are explained, this does not always lead to understanding or improvement. Klein (1990) wrote:

> Although many dyslexics are highly articulate, they often take and use language literally; they do not appear to be able to make the implicit explicit, or know how to get others to do this.

Explanation is an interesting and often difficult area for the dyslexic person. There is an implicit assumption by many people that because an individual possesses a condition they know precisely what to do to fix it. This is in addition to the concept that it can be 'fixed' in the first place. The closest that most people's personal experience comes to that of any disability is illness; but illness, generally speaking, can be treated and ultimately gets better. There is an extrapolated expectation by many individuals that the dyslexic person is in a similar situation, and if only they were able to do the right things the problem would be eliminated.

To a certain extent elimination of as much of the problem as possible is the aim, but 'elimination' is achieved by the introduction and use of strategies that enable coping. The competent dyslexic adult has not cured the problem, but has learned how to bypass and circumvent some of the most obvious difficulties it raises. However, it falls to the lot of the individual to explain this to colleagues and others – including the boss – and once again the onus for containing the difficulty and doing what is necessary falls on to the shoulders of the dyslexic person.

In this respect, the results of a good and complete assessment are frequently invaluable. Psychological assessments to establish the details of the dyslexic person's functioning are relatively common at school level and not infrequent for students at college or university, but it is more rare for adults to need the results of a recent assessment. Nevertheless, such a procedure can provide not only accurate details and information, but can also be useful in providing objective third-party data which may be more readily believed and respected.

It has been stated earlier that the most common conception of what dyslexic means is that it affects reading and writing. This being so, many work colleagues will not be completely surprised at errors in things like spelling or writing, although it is often found that they do expect them to diminish over time. This phenomenon is seen with children, too, and it derives from the fact that most people's experience of not being able to do things leads to the necessity of practice, and if a skill is practised it does tend, usually, to improve. However, although it is true that a great deal of practice may improve the dyslexic person's functioning to a limited degree, lack of practice is not the cause of the problem, and improvement by this route is unlikely. Once again, the task of explaining all this falls upon the shoulders of the dyslexic worker, and once again it is necessary to expose personal difficulties in a public forum.

Earlier in this chapter the difficulty of application forms was discussed. It should be remembered, however, that there are other sorts of forms throughout a great deal of working practice. Many employees are in a position of needing to complete such things as the following:

- order forms
- expenses claim forms
- internal requisitions
- accident record forms
- stock control forms.

People at a more senior level may be provided with more sophisticated forms, such as:

- performance reports
- financial data
- extracts from the customer database
- planning projections
- records of meetings.

This aspect is also frequently complicated by the fact that often such information as financial data is provided at a meeting (with no notice and chance to read it through beforehand) in small, poor quality print from a high-speed printer; this can often mean pages and pages of rows and columns of figures which are supposed to be digested accurately and on the spot!

Apart from these specific situations, practically everyone needs to be able to cope with the following:

- payslips
- tax forms
- holiday records
- important notices
- diaries.

However understandable it is that someone with dyslexia should have difficulties with written material, there is still a level of embarrassment which never goes away entirely. This is important in terms of the individual's self-image, and self-image is important because it permits (or denies) self-respect among colleagues. Each one of us has an 'image' of ourselves within us – that something that each of us recognises as 'me'. Of course it may be true that the image is sometimes out of step with reality, occasionally greatly so, but it is thus that we all manage to cope with our various imperfections and inadequacies on a day-to-day basis. It is, however, important that each one of us has an image that it is possible to live with on a day-to-day basis, and a constant necessity to call this into question, or frequently being reminded that all in the garden is not rosy, will undermine the individual's self-image, self-esteem and self-confidence. If an individual begins to believe that he really is inherently inadequate, he will ultimately behave as if that were true. If that happens, not only will the individual suffer but the employer will not have best service from a valuable employee.

Although practicalities are important, we must not lose sight of the dyslexic person's right of choice. Some situations really are extremely difficult for a particular individual, and the decision that such a situation should be avoided might well be the best way of dealing with it. No one can know that except the dyslexic person, but such a decision can often need negotiation with the boss. This is in itself an anxiety-producing situation for most people, but where the individual can easily appear as if asking for favours or special treatment the stress produced can be high. This must be balanced with the stress produced by continuing to be placed in situations in which it is difficult to function properly, or hard to carry out the task adequately.

Onwards and upwards

As time passes the dyslexic employee, like most others, considers the future; and the future frequently involves some version of promotion.

This immediately raises the spectre of training, examinations and interviews, areas that produce a high level of stress among dyslexic people.

In some respects life becomes easier once the individual becomes more senior. Apart from anything else it is quite likely that there will the provision of a secretary, an assistant or at least access to someone in the typing pool. This means that it is possible that some of the practical tasks can be delegated to another person in whom the dyslexic individual can have confidence, probably with whom some rapport can be established. However, this relationship must be treated very carefully, and there is always the worry that you may be thought stupid or incompetent because you cannot do apparently simple things that a much more junior employee can carry out easily and swiftly. And, of course, this position is usually reached only after considerable time and the acquisition of some seniority. For the working individual starting out on a career life can be very difficult; assistance is frequently needed but by no means always available, and for many people this position necessitates enlisting the help of relatives, family, friends and perhaps work colleagues either to advise or perhaps carry out tasks. This scenario can produce stress on all sides – not just in the dyslexic person. There will be a degree of extra work for the other people, who are helping the dyslexic ones on top of the tasks they already have to do; there will be the necessity of maintaining the relationship, probably with constant explanation about the nature of dyslexia (some people are quite willing to help for a few days or a few weeks, but become puzzled when they realise that this is an ongoing situation), and there may be a degree of 'cover-up' if the dyslexic person is requesting help for things that ought to be done by them and the boss must not find out.

Avoiding tasks that cannot be done, perhaps by seeking out someone else to do them, does not only apply to small day-to-day matters. It is important that employers realise that there is a possibility that a dyslexic employee will avoid larger situations, such as training courses and examinations, which are difficult and do so by not seeking promotion opportunities. It should be the responsibility of the employer under these conditions to monitor progress and discuss the matter with the member of staff if it appears that chances are being turned down. This is not entirely philanthropic, of course, because a better-trained and qualified employee can be of greater benefit to the operation of the enterprise. It does need to be approached sensitively, however, as the idea of training will raise in the minds of many dyslexic people memories of experience at school, which may have established a fairly strong negative attitude to learning. Even in an employee who appears to have confidence, who is good at the job and who generally seems to be coping well, it is frequently true that this is a recent phenomenon. Although such an individual may have confidence and coping skills now, this was by no means always true. Such techniques are learned slowly, and the remembered experience of school and education is that the dyslexic position created stress, and the stress increased errors. As in all of us, the past experience influences present behaviour.

If it is agreed that training is appropriate, practical assistance in coping with the requirements is necessary; how this is done depends on how the training is done, but for internal training opportunities there would be much value in an employer (or the training division of a large company) seeking advice from others who do have experience of the ways in which dyslexic people learn. The dyslexic employee must have support and help throughout the whole process: offering an opportunity is the beginning of the process, not the end.

It is worthwhile for employers to remember that avoiding the difficult tasks is only one side of the coin. The other approach is to look for abilities, rather than disabilities. A person employed and perhaps promoted will have been placed in that position because of things that he or she could do, not in spite of things that he or she could not do. It is valuable to take this concept further. The level of understanding of a dyslexic person is the same as it always would have been; it is the practical aspects of performance that are affected. Therefore, although it is likely to be very hard for them to carry out detailed tasks relating to language and information processing, such as extracting information at speed from complex documents, or correcting drafts of reports, their ability to contribute to wider contexts will be much better. As with all employees, they will function best if placed in a position in which they can utilise their personal abilities, and participation at levels such as policy-making and planning frequently shows a grasp of data not evident in the more mundane tasks.

So where does it all leave us?

Stress is increasingly being recognised as something that must be addressed, and this is true whatever the cause. The fact that in some cases, such as dyslexia, the cause is reasonably obvious can make it easier for everyone, but there is a note of caution here. Where there is an apparently obvious reason for stress it is sometimes too easy to make the link between cause and effect. With a dyslexic employee suffering from stress, there is an obvious assumption that the individual's experience of the combination of the disability and the work environment initiated the stress reaction, and of course this is highly likely to be so in many cases. The fact that it is obvious, however, does not necessarily make it right, and it is important that, especially if the stress symptoms are significant, other possibilities are investigated. These can range from other stress-producing psychological states, other life experiences or even physiological factors such as illness or an incipient tumour.

In practical terms dyslexia is a real disability. However, there are some differences between dyslexia and other disabilities. For one thing it is invisible; it is not alone in this, of course, but there is a tendency for people only to consider things to be 'real' if they can see them. Thus the individual with dyslexia never gets quite the sympathy extended to the blind person or someone in a wheelchair. In some ways the official symbol for disability – the wheelchair – does not always help. Dyslexia also stands out from other types of handicap because of a specific pattern of experience of the problem. In most cases of disability, there is a particular dysfunction which can be diagnosed and specified. The effect of this is to render it impossible – or at least, very difficult – for him to carry out certain tasks, but with the capacity to do things in other fields much the same as it would have been without the problem. Thus the deaf person can do anything that does not require hearing, the blind person can do anything for which sight is not essential, and the individual in a wheelchair can do all those things that do not require walking about. In dyslexia, however, there are important differences. On one hand, the individual has a pattern of difficulties that makes it very difficult (and in some cases even impossible) for him to acquire and use a specific set of skills and, on the other, the manifesting symptoms are those that are frequently seen in other more commonly recognised categories of human functioning: specifically, those who are of low intelligence, have poor skills or are bone idle! This aspect has been recognised for many years, and is commented upon in the Kershaw Report, published in 1974 (Kershaw, 1974).

One aspect that is frequently ignored, or at least given less importance than it should, is that of fatigue. A dyslexic person has to cope with the effects the disability has on functioning, but it is very easy to fall into the trap of believing that this only happens in relation to work, or school, or writing, etc. The organisational inefficiencies in handling information apply to everything in life, of course, and the fatigue arising from it therefore also happens all the time. This aspect of dyslexia is not obvious, but it is important, not least because over time it may have a profound effect on the individual. When someone has to work harder than others to reach the same level in everything, it creates a considerably higher level of pressure and fatigue, and often this is accompanied by the extra burden of being considered not to be working hard enough – or, at least, not as hard as everyone else! This situation is immensely frustrating, and can affect the individual profoundly, and can be a major cause of stress as a component of dyslexia

There are two levels upon which stress in relation to dyslexia may need to be addressed: one of these concerns attempts to alleviate the difficulties engendered by the dyslexia, and the other is in the area of treatment of the stress. For the dyslexic person the two go hand-in-hand and may well both be needed; in both cases it is better to seek professional guidance rather than risk getting it wrong. This does not mean, however, that there is nothing that can be done. Far from it, in most cases much can be done to alleviate the stress arising for the dyslexic individual in the workplace, and, if the stress is eased, then not only is life a good deal better for the individual, but the entire environment becomes a much happier and more productive place for everyone concerned.

What should employers look for?

- Someone who is apparently much more anxious than the job warrants.
- Someone who avoids particular situations, such as never at staff meetings, or never writes memos.
- Any pattern of absenteeism.
- Refusals to take training.
- Unwillingness to consider promotion opportunities.
- A greater level of fatigue than seems to be likely.

Dyslexic employees should do the following:

- Work out the implications of telling people about their dyslexia.
- Plan beforehand how they will explain it and what they will suggest.
- Try to organise their working lives to minimise the most stressful situations.
- Arrange to 'get away' from time to time to consolidate data.
- Realise that stress is involved – not just dyslexia – and learn something about managing it.
- Make sensible choices.
- Seek cooperation and help where necessary: don't be too proud.

Employers of dyslexic employees should do the following:

- Understand that dyslexia is nothing to do with intelligence or ability.
- Realise that some alterations of working practices may be necessary (although these will lead to improved performance).
- Allow time for short breaks to consolidate information.
- Know that for many dyslexic people life and work are a trade-off between speed and accuracy; both are usually not possible at the same time.

Conclusion

There is a great deal of dyslexia about; indeed, as research continues it becomes increasingly apparent that there is probably more in the population than was thought. This means that there is an increasing likelihood that employers will meet dyslexic workers – and indeed most companies probably employ some already, whether they know it or not! We are therefore not addressing a minor difficulty that can be largely ignored, but something that exists in major proportions and affects a substantial part of the adult and working population.

Making proper provision for dyslexic employees is not, therefore, something that is simply good, decent and human, although it is those things, of course. It is something that facilitates the performance of a large number of competent and experienced individuals and enables them not just to work, but to work up to their full potential. In many cases where the dyslexia has not been declared, it may be that the stress symptoms are the first to become apparent, and initially there may be no apparent reason why a particular employee should suffer from stress. There are many reasons for stress, of course, and it is important that all possible causes are investigated. These are not mutually exclusive: in a number of instances there might be a combination of other factors as well as dyslexia.

There have been many myths generated about dyslexic people, but we now know that the truth is that dyslexia is independent of practically every other factor. Dyslexic people are not intellectually deficient, they are not odd and they are by no means inadequate workers. They may have to organise their lives differently from others, but that does not mean that they perform less well. Indeed, in many instances it will be found that the problems that they meet are little different from those met by everyone else – but they are exaggerated and made more obvious.

Some years ago the 'Fit for Work' campaign used the slogan: 'Disabled workers are good workers'. This could easily translate into: 'Dyslexic workers are good workers'. It is much more true, however, if we can make it: 'Stress-free dyslexic workers are very good workers.'

References

Beare D (1975). Self-concept and the adolescent L/LD student. *Journal of Texas Personal and Guidance Association* 4(1): 29–32.

Gauntlett D (1990). Managing the dyslexic adult. In G Hales, M Hales, T Miles, A Summerfield (Eds), *Meeting Points in Dyslexia*. Reading: British Dyslexia Association

Hales G (Ed.) (1994). *Dyslexia Matters*. London: Whurr.

Kershaw J (1974). *People with Dyslexia*. London: British Council for the Rehabilitation of the Disabled.

Klein C (1990). Learning support: A different slant on teaching adult dyslexics. In G Hales, M Hales, T Miles, A Summerfield (Eds), *Meeting Points in Dyslexia*. Reading: BDA.

Selye H (1978). *The Stress of Life*. New York: McGraw-Hill.

Witty P (1950). Reading success and emotional adjustment. *Elementary English* 27: 281–96.

Chapter 7
Stress factors in gifted dyslexic children

PETER CONGDON

Before venturing to consider the nature of stress factors experienced by gifted dyslexic children it may be helpful to clarify the subject of giftedness itself. Briefly, 'gifted' can be used as a general term to cover two major groups of children, namely those of outstanding measured intelligence and those who demonstrate exceptional ability in a particular area. The latter are sometimes referred to as 'talented' children.

High or superior intelligence may refer to those children who, in traditional terminology, record an intelligence quotient in the region of 130 or more. We say 'in the region' of 130 because, even if the notion of a 'quotient' in this sense is legitimate, it would still not be suggested that the figure of 130 should be used as a rigid cut-off point. If, for instance, on a properly administered test of intelligence, a child's profile of scores indicates that he or she is operating in most areas at the 130 IQ level then, in spite of the overall score which may fall somewhat below this level, he or she may well be considered as intellectually gifted. What is important is not the IQ itself but how that global result was arrived at.

Nor should we make the mistake of lumping all children of high or superior intelligence together. There is evidence that individuals scoring in the highest ranges of the intelligence scale, i.e. IQ 150+, may have very special needs. George Bernard Shaw once stated that his education was interrupted by his schooling. Unless we are prepared to consider children of very superior intelligence as special cases then Shaw's criticism may be equally applicable to the education of a very important, if numerically small, group of children in our schools today. We should try to provide for the needs of children of high intelligence and also for those of very high intelligence. However, in the present context, we are not only considering the plight of intellectually gifted children but such children who are also experiencing a degree of dyslexia. Americans sometimes refer to this group as conundrum children or those of dual exceptionality. On the one hand, they have special needs on account of their giftedness and, on the other, they require special attention on account of their learning difficulty.

It is widely agreed that children who experience a degree of dyslexia often demonstrate outstanding abilities in certain areas – in particular spatial, mechanical, constructional and artistic talents; and it has been surmised that such abilities reflect an unusual balance between the two hemispheres of the brain. It is believed that the very dominance of these 'right hemisphere' abilities can result in a corresponding depression of the language abilities which depend on the opposite or left hemisphere. Dyslexia can be seen, therefore, to arise from a brain difference rather than from a brain defect.

A number of researches both in Britain and abroad have highlighted a particular pattern of scores which dyslexics often manifest on the Wechsler Children's Intelligence Scale (Wechsler, 1992). The pattern is sometimes referred to as the ACID profile. The four letters A, C, I and D refer to the initial letters of the Wechsler sub-tests Arithmetic, Coding, Information and Digit Span. If an individual records low scores on these tests relative to her or his other scores then it may result from the fact that she or he is experiencing difficulties in coping with certain aspects of language. His Arithmetic may be low because he suffers from the problem of dealing with symbolic language. His score on the Coding test may be low because this measure demands automatic responses to arbitrary symbols, and this is very similar to what is demanded by reading and spelling. He records a low score on Information because basically this is a general knowledge test and development in this area may have been depressed by poor literacy skills. Finally, the Digit Span score may be low because this is a measure of the ability to remember items in sequence – another ability that is crucial to the processes involved in mastery of written language.

When considering the overall depressing effect that scores on certain sub-tests may have on a child's global IQ, then an examination of the scores on the other tests becomes imperative as a possible indicator of the child's intellectual potential. It is this very examination that can highlight the intricate way in which dyslexia and giftedness are often related.

In a study of 160 cases of dyslexia (Congdon, 1989) it was discovered that of the 115 whose Verbal or Performance IQs did not reach the superior level, no less than 36 (29 male, 7 female) recorded scores on three or more sub-tests which were equivalent to superior scores. Of these 36 some 15 in fact recorded scores on four or more sub-tests at the superior level. These findings, therefore, not only further confirm the existence of the many exceptional intellectual abilities to be found in a population of dyslexic subjects, but also highlight the kind of pressures such individuals experience in the development of their functional intelligence. It is common for a dyslexic to show an uneven profile of abilities. For a gifted dyslexic this very unevenness may be of exceptional proportions and cause correspondingly greater disturbance in both the child's mental and emotional growth.

A wintry climate of opinion

The gifted and the dyslexic have often been faced with what can only be termed a 'wintry climate of opinion', and this arises from a general failure to understand the two conditions. In the past, dyslexia has been misconstrued as a middle-class syndrome or an excuse for low ability or poor motivation. Giftedness has equally been misunderstood. There has been a general failure to identify and stretch the abilities of gifted children, and the attitude that such children have been born with a silver spoon in their mouths and should learn that they are not the only pebble on the beach has been prevalent in a society that glorifies the average. The situation can become particularly stressful for an otherwise highly intelligent child who is experiencing problems with basic reading, spelling and writing, and who is largely judged on the standard of these. The gifted and the dyslexic have been among the most neglected in our educational system and the child who falls in both categories may be at a total loss.

Preschool and infants: the signs emerge

Many gifted children appear as preschool children to be bright and alert and able in all kinds of areas, and their parents, who may feel at times that something is not quite as it should be, nevertheless assume that the child will make progress when schooling begins. With such children valuable time has often already been lost before they go to school.

Some parents may have tried teaching their otherwise bright child with conventional methods which may have brought success with other siblings but which now appear to produce few positive results. The lack of success with the written word, even at this very early stage, can produce the beginnings of an aversion towards the subject. Parents may well blame themselves as being inadequate in the teaching process and feel that all will be well when the child goes to school. Years later when they learn about the condition of dyslexia, they may recall these early failures.

Until they start school intellectually gifted children have every reason to believe that they are perfectly normal and at least the equal of their contemporaries. Many have been well ahead of their peers in language, in walking and in general social development. Some may have astounded adults with their precocity in certain spheres. Then suddenly these children come face to face with inferiority and failure in an aspect of life that appears to be important for reasons that they cannot understand. Reactions can vary. Some lose interest and adopt negative and avoidance attitudes. Others may try harder, spurred on by their teacher and parents, only to discover that the greater effort does not produce the longed for results. A feeling of disillusionment and mystification sets in. Until then the child had been told he was clever and he believed it. Now he develops doubts in himself. The teacher's attitude may not help. As most intelligent children learn to read quickly, it is all too easy for the teacher to infer that the child who conspicuously fails to read is either lazy or dull, in spite of a superficial brightness. In the former case, with the child being driven beyond his capacity, there is little hope of developing a constructive relationship between teacher and child, and both soon find themselves at cross-purposes. In the latter case, the child may be written off as not worth a great deal of trouble. The preschool or infant stage can witness the emergence of attitudes that can affect the child's development for the rest of his school career and beyond.

Transfer to the junior stage

By the time the child transfers to the junior stage of education, he may already have been tagged with the 'lazy' or 'dull' label. It is at this stage that the educational pressures begin to increase with more emphasis on the 3 Rs and in many places the 11+ examination is still casting its shadow. It is also at this level that self-awareness begins to show and young gifted children are often precocious in this respect. The failing reader not only has to cope with his own self-doubt but also with the knowledge that poor progress 'far from being a secret shame, often becomes a public failure' (Gaines, 1989, quoted by Pumfrey and Reason, 1991). For the gifted dyslexic who previously may have had high aspirations for himself, this period may be particularly traumatic. Like any other children with learning problems he may act out in a variety of ways. These may take the form of temper tantrums, aggression or destructiveness. Many gifted children want perfection and are satisfied with nothing less. If they cannot reach the high standards they set themselves, they sometimes destroy what attempts they have made or refuse to participate in the activity any longer. Some retreat into themselves or resort to day-dreaming or 'playing dumb'. Other manifestations of emotional disturbance arising from the problem are enuresis, stammer, sleep-walking, asthma and various physical symptoms, such as vomiting and recurrent abdominal pains for which no physical cause can be found. The situation is not helped when attempts are made to treat the secondary symptom rather than the primary cause, which is an underlying learning difficulty.

As a result of the various pressures on them, together with their continued failure in basic scholastic subjects, many intellectually gifted children who are also dyslexic have little idea of the extent of their high intellectual potential. This has become only too apparent to me and, as an educational psychologist specialising in the assessment of such children, I have noted their responses to such questions as, 'Did you know that you have high ability?' or 'Did you know that you have high intelligence?'. Some would beam and reply 'Yes, I am good at this, that or the other'. Many, however, would react with confusion and disbelief and reply, 'So I am not thick or stupid' or words to that effect. Responses of this nature remind us that there is little systematic documentation of the views and feelings of dyslexic children themselves. Publications tend to concentrate on personal accounts by dyslexic adults or on parents' descriptions of the plight of their children.

Parental pressures

The parents of young gifted children often, and not unreasonably, have high aspirations for them. They see their offspring as superior to, or well above, the average and not unexpectedly anticipate a high standard of attainment when they enter school. When this is not forthcoming the disappointment and disillusionment can be traumatic for both parent and child. Nor is parental distress necessarily proportional to the extent of the disability. This may relate to values, ambitions, hopes and knowledge (Knusson and Cunningham, 1988). I have known parents dismiss serious cases of dyslexia whereas others will over-react to mild or moderate cases. When their child fails to live up to expectations the disappointment can be marked.

Reactions towards school and the education system also differ. Although some parents accept their child's shortcomings and its consequent effects, others automatically blame the teachers and so deny that necessary collaboration which is an indispensable requisite to their child's education. Gifted dyslexic children can find themselves under a particular strain. Many of their outstanding abilities are recognised by their parents but ignorance concerning the condition of dyslexia can result in those same parents becoming vexed, angry and unkind towards the child whom they see as careless and poorly motivated. Some children are the victims of bullying by disappointed fathers. At the other end of the scale, excessive anxiety on the part of loving and caring parents can have equally adverse effects. The children may react by attention-seeking behaviour. Too often they become aggressive and antisocial. It is of interest to note that a large proportion of juvenile delinquents have reading and spelling difficulties, and many of these have undisclosed talents in certain areas.

Transfer to secondary school

Late identification compounds emotional problems. Often the child's learning difficulties are not recognised until late in the primary stage of education. This is frequently so with the gifted dyslexic who may be adept at employing other abilities to compensate for or to cloak inadequacies with written language. By the time the problem is recognised and remedial help is beginning to take effect, the child is then faced with the traumatic experience of being transferred to a secondary school. The secondary school may be much larger and impersonal and the curriculum is more formal and demanding. It thereby places an extra strain on what are precisely the child's weak points, namely reading, writing and organisational skills. This is the time when new subjects and new areas of knowledge are introduced. The learning of foreign languages takes on greater importance. An intellectually gifted child normally approaches such a time with enthusiasm and interest. However, for one who has a history of dyslexia, this stage may mean only more frustration, more failure and, in some cases, more exposure to ridicule.

It is at the secondary level that emotional symptoms and behavioural disorders arising from an underlying learning problem often take on a more antisocial form. Truancy, not unknown at the junior level, becomes more prevalent and the same is true of stealing, pathological lying and the drift into more destructive gang activities. For particularly sensitive individuals, deep emotional disturbance, depression, fantasy-building and other neurotic signs are manifested. Adolescence with all its turmoil is enough without the extra problem of dyslexia. However, the outlook need not be completely bleak for the adolescent. At this level many discover for the first time that they are dyslexic and they experience a sense of relief when it is explained to them. Yet coupled with the sense of relief there may also be an element of despair, anger and bewilderment. The intellectually gifted child may experience a deep sense of injustice. Being aware of the responsibilities of those in charge of his education, he may well ask, 'Why didn't the school or the local education authority identify the problem before and arrange appropriate help?'.

Dyslexic children who come from families who view school involvement as of little consequence may happily contract out of any attempt to achieve. Such children may find that, although they cannot become literate, there are other socially acceptable school or out-of-school activities and they concentrate on becoming competent in these. Gifted athletes, musicians, artists and builders are to be found in this group.

Towards the end of their schooling it is natural for children to look forward to what will happen when they leave school. As intellectually gifted individuals they might legitimately have anticipated a demanding and stimulating career. The knowledge that this may now be barred from them owing to their problems with basic literacy is likely to produce anxiety and frustrations, and increase emotional tensions, and these can be exacerbated by the realisation that they are disappointing their parents' career expectations for them. For many technical and virtually all 'white collar' jobs, some evidence of having passed examinations is required. This may well be merely a routine and the employer may well set little store by it. However, the candidate who has no certificate to produce may be deterred from applying. When he does make an application he is likely to be asked to do so in writing. Whether this is done on a prescribed form or in a letter of his own composition, he will find it difficult to present himself in the best light. He will be vulnerable to revealing the limitations of his literacy skills and his educational attainments, and it is these which, in the public mind, are normally associated with ability. The gifted dyslexic like any other will be at risk of being eliminated before she or he is considered for interview.

For those dyslexic individuals who are able to take written examinations, it is fair to say that they can now be offered special consideration or dispensation. This may take the form of extra time or having someone read the question to them. However, there are some who choose not to take advantage of such arrangements. Some may see it as an unfair advantage over other candidates with whom they wish to compete on equal terms. Others are dissuaded on account of the fact that details of the dispensation may appear on any certificate that they may be awarded, and this would therefore reduce its value.

Management

Careful management is essential for all dyslexic children if they are to reach their potential, and this is especially so for gifted dyslexic children, who may have much to offer in a wide variety of areas and yet whose limitations with written language may hold them back with tragic results. To prevent this happening, early identification and appropriate help are essential. Ideally this should be done either at the preschool level or when the child first enters school. It is unrealistic to talk about a 'cure' for dyslexia but a great deal can be done to help the child reach a standard in written communication which will facilitate progress in other areas.

It is paramount that parents, teachers and the child should work together in an atmosphere of trust. Gifted children are often capable of a high level of understanding of a problem at a comparatively young age. It can be explained to them how it is possible to be clever in many ways and yet still have difficulty with reading and spelling. Often the diagnosis of dyslexia and the use of the term itself can be helpful in making it easier for both parents and child to come to terms with the negative aspects. For the parents it offers reassurance that no shortcomings on their part have been responsible for the child's difficulties, whereas the children recognise that they are not just 'dull' or 'lazy'. Susan Hampshire, the gifted actress, writes:

> If I had known what was the matter with me and why I couldn't read, would everything have been easier just because my difficulties had a name? Yes, it would. To know that it was not a disease but a disability, a condition that could be improved, would have made all the difference.

Hampshire (1981)

The guide *Dyslexia: Towards a Better Understanding* (Congdon, 1981) was purposely written to help young able dyslexic children to understand their learning difficulty. It is written in the first person in simple conversational language and contains many cartoon-like illustrations together with examples of famous people who were dyslexic.

Opportunities should be given for allowing the use of alternative means of communication wherever possible. This can include oral or spoken language as well as the use of up-to-date technology. Many dyslexic children show an aptitude for computers and word processors and this should be exploited by offering early training in touch typing.

The possibility of help in alleviating the condition of dyslexia provides an optimistic outlook. What one can hope to achieve can be substantial and for the intellectually gifted and talented, who can compensate in all sorts of ways, the future can indeed be bright. For such children, like any others, it is important to emphasise their strengths while not overlooking their weaknesses.

References

Congdon PJ (1981). *Dyslexia: Towards a Better Understanding*. Solihull: GCIC.

Congdon PJ (1989). *Dyslexia: A Pattern of Strengths and Weaknesses*. Solihull: GCIC.

Gaines K (1989). The use of reading diaries as a short term intervention strategy. *Reading* 23(3): 141–5.

Hampshire S (1981). *Susan's Story*. London: Sidgwick & Jackson.

Knusson C, Cunningham CC (1988) Stress, disability and handicap. In S Fisher, J Reason (Eds). *Handbook of Life Stress, Cognition and Health*. Chichester: Wiley.

Pumfrey PD, Reason R (1991). *Specific Learning Difficulties* (Dyslexia). London: Routledge.

Wechsler D (1992). *Wechsler Children's Intelligence Scale*. Sidcup: The Psychological Corporation.

Chapter 8
Stress factors within the family

ROGER SAUNDERS*

Indeed when there is a 'dyslexic in the house' it can create considerable stress. At times these feelings can become so immobilising that the family becomes near the familiar 'dysfunctioning stage'. At other times, in contrast, a mild-to-moderate reaction can mobilise the family around 'the cause' and bring all the members into a more harmonious relationship.

Several factors come to mind to create the degree of stress in the dyslexic family: the age of the person (child or adult) when first discovered, the facilities for educational treatment, and the 'excess emotional baggage' which the various members of the family have endured before the awareness of dyslexia as an added 'burden'. For example, for whatever reasons, a marriage that has been strained for years can be unable to cope further with the necessary requirements that the dyslexic condition in one or more members of the family can necessitate. Moreover, in some instances the re-education process can take so long and be so arduously demanding that the parents' patience can be tested to the limit.

Having been involved in the field of dyslexia for well over 40 years, the writer chooses to share personal experiences which he has known, clinically, from many families, many of whom have been followed from childhood, through marriage, to their own children, creating a 'third

*The author apologises for the reference to the masculine. The use of 'he or she', 'him or her' seems grammatically clumsy and boring to the reader. Although statistics may be changing, it is generally assumed that in the population of dyslexics there are four times as many boys as girls. It is hoped that none of the female dyslexics has been offended by this masculine reference. They are just as important, and at times, because of fewer girls with the problem, can experience even greater stress. Although I have no hard evidence I have often felt that if it is the mother who is dyslexic there can be greater stress in the family. The mother, often because of her freer work schedule, is the parent who initially goes to the school for conferences. Entering the educational institution or building, a black cloud of memories of early fears and frustration can descend, reducing the mother to being unable to communicate appropriately. The administrators and teachers observe her high level of anxiety and unknowingly remark, 'No wonder the child is upset, look how anxious the mother is'.

generation' of data from observations. Some attempt will be made to classify the traditional family constellations and their reactions to stress. These categories will range from the involvement of the grandparents, the parents, their children, the child and/or his siblings.

Grandparents

A grandmother often feels that the daughter-in-law had turned a 'deaf ear' to her as she tried to share some of her own early experiences encountered in rearing the child's father. The grandmother's memory may be remarkably challenged and brought back to light when she observes her grandchild's learning style, or specifically the non-learning of critical skills. She well remembers their startled reaction when a highly verbal child began to fall behind and/or to exhibit significant symptoms which were later classified as 'dyslexia'. Now armed with all of that wisdom, she is aware of the possibility of a genetic link between her husband's style of learning and that of her son and that of her grandson. Her daughter-in-law might subtly or overtly refuse the grandparent's concern and send the message 'Don't butt in'. The daughter-in-law can be blinded by these warning signals because she only observes her very successful husband (and father-in-law) and has no clue to the personal history of how his parents had met the challenge of his educational needs in youth. The grandmother's intent, remembering her husband's and son's experience, is to 'soften' the emotional response to the frightening evidence when her grandson exhibits similar patterns knowing that very special needs must be met head-on. Tact and diplomacy on the part of the grandparents are crucial to keep the 'lines of communication' open and to avoid being 'tuned out' by those who need to listen the most.

Parents

When the couple first met, courted and were married, the father's painful emotional scars of the past were possibly well healed. Moreover, anxieties had been reduced and the stress of those earlier years forgotten. On the other hand, his wife might have observed that when her husband is under some experience requiring the use of reading, and particularly expository writing, he can become anxious. Not uncommon is an out-of-character 'blow up' exhibited when he innocently asks her how to spell a word and she retorts, 'Look it up', or 'I spelled it for you yesterday, why can't you remember it?'. She is not aware that these are continued symptoms of his dyslexic learning condition and the residual feelings of stress encountered from his early educational years.

Living with a dyslexic child, who, in spite of the parents' best efforts, continues to fail can gradually become more and more stressful until the reality of the learning style has been properly addressed by a professional diagnosis. Before this discovery the parents have struggled with their youngster without being mindful of the unique characteristics or the style of a dyslexic learner. Usually they have been discouraged with the child and have run the gamut of questions: 'Is it our fault?', 'What have we done wrong?', 'Why can't he learn?', 'Why is our adorable child having a personality change – for the worse . . .?' Searching for answers, naturally they have turned to educational administrators and teachers with whom to share their dilemma. Seeing the frustrations of the parents, the teachers attempt to deal with the parents' feelings, fears and anxieties, *rather* than looking closely at the child and searching for clues as to what is really wrong. Example after example springs to mind, particularly of the child who is reasonably successful in the early grades, but, when the academic demands for reading and writing and comprehension become greater, can gradually begin to fall behind. Uninformed teachers blame either *external* or *internal* factors for a child's failure to learn.

The *external factors* are when the blame is placed on the external environment, such as: 'The parents are not supportive', 'The parents are expecting too much', 'There is too much confusion at home', 'The parents are stressing other things more than academics, such as sports, drama, art, music, etc.', 'The parents need better control of their children.'

As for the *internal factors*, the child is blamed, with statements such as: 'He doesn't pay attention consistently', 'He's too involved in other activities (sports, girls, car repairs, etc.)', or 'He is unmotivated, lazy, emotionally immature, etc.'. Blaming the external and internal factors, and communicating these with the parents, does little to reduce the stress which parents feel when the child continues to fail. Usually it increases the guilt, as when one mother of a dyslexic son was blamed for influencing and/or damaging her developing fetus because she stretched and hung draperies during the sixth month of pregnancy. Seldom does the teacher look at the educational 'system' and place blame thereon, and certainly she does not heap stress and guilt on herself, by exclaiming, 'Not my fault, I am a certified teacher', 'I have had good training, and the other children are responding well to my teaching strategies'. Therefore, the stress intensifies until proper recognition that this is a child with learning patterns that are different from the norm.

In some families this scenario is not as stressful because, in some instances, it is not unusual for parents to have had some awareness of the nature of dyslexia; therefore, when symptoms first occur they quickly search for realistic explanations of the child's failure. Although the stress factor in this case is limited, concern and stress do occur when parents ponder about, 'What's going to happen in the future?', and, in particular, when they cannot find adequate educational facilities to offer some 'prevention' of the symptoms before they become crippling or undermine proper educational growth. Moreover, parents might have learned from their own experiences and their observations of other children, as well as their neighbours' children and their siblings' children. Hopefully, emphasis on public awareness of the early signs of dyslexia, or that it 'runs in families' (the genetic cause), has allowed parents to observe other children who have shown some delay in the acquisition of language at an early stage, and wonder what lies ahead. Even 'non-verbal' children have forewarned their parents to be more or less prepared for this dilemma of achievement in the more formalised teaching experiences. Moreover, they have been aware that a child has shown less interest in 'books', or in learning the alphabet, and sometimes a delay in the efficient use of the pencil and/or crayons. On the other hand, they have also seen extraordinary strength in the manipulation of visual–spatial relationships, such as taking toys apart and putting them back together, extreme creativity in building with blocks, talents in motor coordination, music, dance, and other strengths that are out of harmony with the lack of interest in the educational routines, and demonstrate much higher talent than their same age peers.

Marion Welchman, of the British Dyslexia Association, has in her lectures clearly illustrated what happens within the family and with the siblings when one sibling has the dyslexic condition. First she draws a circle on the board and says, 'This is the normal family circle, all living in harmony with each other'. Then she draws a little hump on the circle and says, 'This represents one sibling who has dyslexia, undiagnosed'. Then as she begins to talk about the necessary management and attention required to address the needs of the dyslexic child's problems, this 'hump' becomes larger and larger, and pretty soon is in itself as large as the family circle. This clearly illustrates the tension that can be created in the family when the parents must begin to focus more and more on the sibling (or siblings) who have a different learning style.

The parents must also face the financial burden which, in itself, adds additional stress to the family's budget, and face the burden of scheduling for extra time for homework, extra trips to the tutor, etc., and the list becomes never ending.

Sib-ship stress

With the more affluent families, the parents may enrol their child in a school the curriculum of which is designed especially for the dyslexic learner. This can create great sibling rivalry, because these schools have built into their philosophy and curriculum the idea that one of the *first steps towards rehabilitation* is to create an environment in which the child becomes a successful and enthusiastic learner. This can create disharmony with a sibling who is struggling with the traditional educational system which lacks creativity and personal attention. Many extremely gifted siblings could certainly profit from the type of originality or creativity involved in the dyslexic educational system; however, unless the public school has 'classes for the gifted', these children go with their needs unmet and can become sour and less enthusiastic about educational pursuits – jealous of their sibling.

Another condition which becomes more and more stressful to the dyslexic student is when a sibling, 2 or 3 years younger, equally as bright and linguistically facile, exhibits none of the typical dyslexic symptoms, sits quietly, observing the teaching of his dyslexic sibling during the homework period or during tutoring, and begins to 'catch on' to reading quite spontaneously. This puts the older sibling's 'nose out of joint'. Parents struggle to give 'equal time', but this is difficult because they are aware that the older child has greater specific needs for survival in the educational system than the younger child. Even grandparents can begin to favour the dyslexic child, trying to ease burdens for the entire family by remembering when they had walked in the same footsteps of the parents in the years passed.

Stress reducers

The greatest stress reducer comes after the awareness of the condition, when the child, with the proper teaching, begins to learn. Although this might occur quickly, it may take longer. It is not uncommon for the parents to recognise that not only is the child making academic progress, but, as many, many have exclaimed, 'Thank goodness, we've got our little boy back'. This means that the therapeutic intervention in the academic area has also resolved some of the fears and frustrations (and *stress*) which the child was feeling as a result of academic failure. Actually, many untrained teachers continue to 'pound away' at teaching strategies that are *inappropriate*, and the dyslexic child has begun to experience what I term 'academic abuse'.

The awareness of the dyslexic learning 'condition' is the first step leading towards the proper treatment. This comes about through diagnosis by an experienced clinician. The in-depth discussion should help to erase the 'bad labels', or blame, of the external and internal accusations.

The diagnostic process should not be hurried as it can be for a minor medical problem. For example, in a very short time a paediatrician can see a 'red throat' and give an appropriate prescription. However, the diagnosis of dyslexia, at whatever age, starts with an explanation of the strength and weaknesses from the traditional intellectual assessment. This should be explained thoroughly. Often a 'visual' is helpful. The clinician draws the graph of the intelligence test, labelling 'average, above average, superior, below average', etc. Also, it helps to draw a traditional bell-shaped curve marking these categories while placing the 'grade levels' underneath. This shows the discrepancy between where a child with normal learning ability would be placed and the levels achieved by the dyslexic. For example, a child in the third grade with superior intelligence should be reading at around sixth grade or higher, whereas the dyslexic's reading may be barely 'grade level'. From personal experience I believe that the strengths of the dyslexic are usually in the cognitive, 'thinking' areas, such as commonsense reasoning (comprehension), abstract thinking (similarities) and possibly oral vocabulary development. The non-verbal tasks which require the manipulation of visual–spatial materials can also be a strength. The explanation of the differences in the memory system can help a child understand his dyslexic style of learning. An extremely important part of this evaluation is the in-depth family history. Examining arduously the levels of achievement of parents, uncles, aunts, cousins, etc. can bring relief to a puzzled child, because, when he hears that his favourite uncle or highly admired first cousin is also dyslexic, he gains courage to feel that his future is bright. The thrust of such an interview should be explained in the language the child understands and the intent of the outcome should be that the child leaves the office feeling, 'It's not my fault'.

As Margaret Byrd Rawson (Editor Emeritus of *Annals of Dyslexia*, published by the Orton Dyslexia Society) says, 'Diagnosis without treatment is criminal'. Therefore the next step in reducing the often blinding stress is an educational prescription that addresses the 'different' learning style. Available facilities for this prescription may vary. Some local public educational facilities are able to accept a diagnosis and deal appropriately with the child's needs. However, most are not. Therefore the parent must search for other resources. Private tutoring in or out of school, home teaching or a transfer to a school (boarding or an independent day school) specialising in the education of the dyslexic child can be an option. Finances play a big part in this selection, as mentioned earlier. This added burden, while reducing the stress on the dyslexic student, can shift some additional stress to the family's lifestyle, perhaps limiting lengthy vacations or family excursions, etc.

Answers to the unanswered questions 'How long will he need help?', 'Will he make college?', 'What of his employment future?' can be a *stress reducer* if the clinician has years of experience and can assure the parents of other children, who, when given proper day-by-day management, have succeeded. Rawson (1995) is very reassuring for parents pondering these questions. Also parents must be reassured that they *can have confidence in their own judgement* because they have proved their adequacy as parents by having searched arduously for the right answers to their original question of 'Why can't he learn like others?'. Hearing this from a professional lowers their fears and anxieties about, 'What of the future?'.

Magnifying strengths is a 'must' for preserving the integrity and 'self-opinion' of the dyslexic at any age. 'What are you good at?' is often a surprise question because the child has had teachers who only observed and mentioned what he is 'bad at'. Learning that because one is a 'bad speller' does not make one a 'bad person' is the message to get across.

Often the financial stress can be reduced by the parents searching for opportunities for earning additional income. Also, learning how to help other dyslexics by taking courses for tutors or teachers has helped many mothers to have greater insight into her child's dilemma about learning. As one socially prominent mother said, 'I am tired of pouring pink tea at the women's socials; I would like to learn how to help my Johnny and many others like him'. And she did – and many other mothers joined in 'the cause' from her enthusiasm which gradually led to the formation of a local branch of the Orton Dyslexia Society, to a special summer camp, to college courses for teacher's credit and to an international conference on the topic of dyslexia. A recent newsletter from a school in Seattle, Washington, which specialises in the education of dyslexic children, quoted a letter from a mother:

> No one knows better than me the value of education and the cost of not achieving one, and there's no price I can put on the education he is receiving at [his present school]. For a child like him it is truly a gift of life, a chance to succeed and hope to overcome nearly insurmountable barriers.

Many mothers overcome the long-standing guilt that they have borne for feeling that they were at fault, by shifting their stress energy into a more productive experience through becoming active in organisations devoted to furthering the understanding of dyslexia. Parents can be 'movers and shakers' when their purpose is just and clearly defined.

Reducing stress in relationship to one's employment also requires understanding and management. For example, the bright, creative, personable, likeable employee who is advancing up the 'company ladder' may be frightened that the next step up is a 'desk job', which places great emphasis on reading and writing. In many such instances, the selection of a competent secretary has allowed the freedom for him to continue in his area of strengths and expertise and not be hampered by the 'paper and pencil work'.

Often parents reduce their stress over the fear of job inadequacy by magnifying their own strengths or, if possible, by becoming employed in their area of strength, such as building, selling, designing or gravitating towards jobs that rely on good 'personality' traits rather than those demanding academic prowess. Off-duty recreational activities such as sports, gardening, home repairs, etc., or pursuing talents in art, music, design, etc., have been a 'saving factor' to many parents burdened with the stress of living in a dyslexic family.

Studying the lives of past and current successful and famous dyslexics is important. Lloyd Thomson's (1969) article can be a great boost to dyslexics fearful of their future. One dyslexic teacher developed a question and answer format in which she listed the accomplishments of these great people and had the students guess whom this referred to. Currently, seldom does a day go by that one does not hear of a successful dyslexic who has just 'come out of the closet'.

In summary, stress in the family is a real emotional experience for everybody. Stepping stones taken one-at-a-time can keep stress from becoming an insurmountable 'stumbling block' to the future of the dyslexic learner and his family.

References

Rawson MB (1995). *Dyslexia Over the Life Span: A Fifty-five-year Longitudinal Study*. Cambridge, MA: Educators Publishing Service.

Thomson L (1969). Language disabilities in men of eminence. *Bulletin of the Orton Society* 19: 113–18.

Chapter 9
The dyslexics speak for themselves

MICHAEL NEWBY, JOY ALDRIDGE, BROTHER MATTHEW
SASSE, SHEENA HARRISON and JANET COKER

Michael Newby

The various signs associated with dyslexia often give rise to feelings of
deficiency, long before the individual reaches school. I can remember
being troubled, as an infant, by such things as being behind my peers in
playing games requiring coordination. Such feelings of deficiency intensify when adults express concern about such initial difficulties. If adults
subsequently strongly encourage dyslexics into areas of compensatory
activities, then this can increase a child's stress as deficiency motivations
become suppressed.

Dyslexia 2000 (1994) gives prominence to 'Comments which make
your Blood Boil'.* These fully illustrate the depth of feelings still around
in adult dyslexics by negative comments, as well as indicating problems
with self-esteem. Our depths of feeling usually derive from childhood
experiences. At school such negative comments led me to truant
frequently. In later years my own children had to face such negatives but
never truented. I built up their confidence by telling them their initial
difficulties were signs of being a cygnet not an 'Ugly Duckling', and that
trying was more important than the marks they obtained. Not that they
completely escaped stress: Claire, normally well behaved at school,
threw ink over the teacher who said she would never pass an exam. With
encouragement she, like Simon, kept on trying even when the Maths
Dept. gave up trying to teach her.

Widening my children's interests aided them to avoid most of the
pressure inflicted by a linear system of education, which imposes
constraints on those who think in other ways. This also helped them to
become highly adaptive. Simon, despite low 'A' level passes, within a year
of leaving school was put in charge of an experienced team dealing with

*Such comments include, 'You can't be dyslexic if you can read all right – you just have a prob-
lem with your spelling'; 'I have a bad memory too – that does not make me dyslexic', and 'It's
just a fancy name for people who are lazy and don't want to learn' [editors].

105

severely maladjusted children. A few years later, after several more promotions, he resigned in protest at a policy of cuts which actually harmed such vulnerable children. He is now a super-market manager. Claire surprised her school by passing 12 GCSEs including Maths. She is now both a qualified nurse and primary teacher.

Both Claire and I were placed under stress at teacher training college by tutors stating that dyslexics should never be admitted to college. A view now held by government, who have officially undervalued the potential of such dyslexics as poor spellers. Although I started off teaching Art, my main area of compensatory activity, I soon began publishing work in my areas of deficiency and ended up a Head of Science and Computing. My daughter, after out-performing her college tutors in some Maths areas, now takes a remedial group for Maths and runs an Art club, also a subject in which she felt deficient, on top of her normal class teaching.

All of us find that conflicting signals get in our way in such areas as spelling. Stress can arise in dyslexics because they tend to use more than one strategy in order to cope with malsequencing.* Out of sequence signals, as well as restructuring the data symbols which are essential for innovative thought, also produce the misspellings and other signs which are likewise creative, but unacceptable, responses. Strategies and malsequenced signals can therefore clash and both can generate stress. Moreover, when such automatic restructuring escapes control, it can lead either to deep daydreaming or to mental confusion; both of which can interfere with effective cognition. This in turn very often leads to stress.

The encouragement of wide interests usually results in greater richness of strategies, which help to prevent such consequences. Enrichment is essential in the education of dyslexics. For example poetry writing can use emotions creatively and ecology provides live examples of net diagrams for non-linear thinkers. Even being allowed a different way of keeping possessions can help, since such thinkers often try to lay things out in a way that reflects their inner storage of information. To impose linear tidiness upon dyslexics often leads to stress as it conflicts with their own logic. The linearly neat dyslexics I know have all turned out to be bad managers of their lives, whilst the so-called scatter brains in our family all seem to reach senior positions and see dyslexia as indicating potentiality not disability (compare West, 1991).

References

Adult Dyslexia Organisation (1994). Comments that make your blood boil. *Dyslexia 2000* 2 (1): 2. Published by the Adult Dyslexia Organisation, 336 Brixton Road, London SW9 7AA.

West TG (1991). *In the Mind's Eye*. Buffalo, NY: Prometheus Books.

*Michael Newby, in a personal communication to the editors, has argued that the word 'malsequencing' aptly describes the distinctive difficulties of the dyslexic [editors].

Joy Aldridge: Disruptive dyslexic cycle of stress

I feel a small 'pen-sketch' of my dyslexic background may be of help to the reader I am in my fourties, born after the war into a poor working class farming family, the middle of seven children. My early educational life was traumatic and stressful. My older sister had the unenvible task of 'dragging' me by the hand to school. She has often recounted the day I sat in the middle of the main road causing the stoppage of lorries and cars. Due to my social/class background the teachers expectation of my ability and performance was low to say the least. So no one seemed to care that I had great difficulty with learning to read and write which personally caused me a great deal of unhappiness and distress. With the net result that I went through my school years and early adult life with a poor self image and low self esteem and being extremely shy. However, I did excell on the sports field. That I left school at fifteen with no academic paper-work was of little surprise or concern to anyone but my self. What followed was low paid work and latter marriage.

On the death of my beloved father, with two children (my son was experiencing specific language problems, having not said baby sounds until the age of three) I wished to know more about my fathers experience in the war, to which end I enrolled in an 'O' level modern history class, with no thoughts of taking the exam, just to gain an understanding. I got carried away with the flow of the class and managed a 'O'. Having made friends with another mature student at her persuasion I enrolled in english language gaining a 'B' which equally surprised the tutor and myself. I don't think any exam result will ever taste as sweet as that one. Sociology 'O' and 'A' level followed, with the teacher in the sociology class advising me that the way my mind worked I might be more suited to degree level study. The advise coincided with the need and desire to find out more about language and the learning process to help understand my sons learning needs. At the time of this advice and when dispairing of ever getting the appropriate help at school for my son who by now was six years old, I stumbled by chance on a book by Tim Miles about Dyslexia. Up to this point in time I had not been aware of dyslexia. Autisum had been rulled out and he had been diagnosed as suffering from a specific language disorder. On completion of the book I paid to have a full assessment for my son. When in receipt of the report I gave a copy to the schools educational psychologist, only to have the report thrown back at me across the table with the words 'it's irresponsible for someone to write a report like this of someone so young', by now he was seven. My behaviour that followed and the resulting advised changed the path of my son's life and my own. I wrote to Tim Miles, sending a copy of the report. Tim replied, gave me his home phone number and during the course of two phone calls gave me guidance and advice in respect to what I could do to help improve my son's present circumstances and that which would help him to reach his potential. To this day, I and My son owe Tim Miles a great debt, the like of which can't be repaid.

I enrolled with the Open University, not with the aim of gaining a degree, just to gain what knowledge I could. One day towards the end of the course, I took a step back and looked long and hard at the Tutors comments and ask my self 'was it possible that I too could be dyslexic?'. Once the question of my own dyslexia had come to rest in my conciousness I needed to find out the truth about myself. To which end I again wrote to Tim Miles in North Wales to ask if he would be prepared to do an assessment.

On a damp autumn day before the break of dawn I journed from Reading Station to North Wales. The person who made the journey down was not the same person who returned the early hours of the following day, a few days away from my first of many O.U. exams. I remember Tim being just as pleased with his results as I. I recall his looking around the room and pointing to his books linning one wall and saying 'if you had not been dyslexic you could have achieved this', his advise being to grow a tough hide and study to the level I felt I could cope with given the level I was reading and spelling at. Before I left Dorthy Gilroy gave me some very valuable advice too and has kept in touch over the years encouraging me. With out such commited people, many of us dyslexics would still be perishing by the wayside of academic life. I still have the study bug, I am still studing with the Open University. I don't know if I will ever catch up the lost days of learning.

As a post script, my son has just turned nineteen. After being told at the age of four and a half that he would not do well at 'normal' school and being informed that ESN school might suit him better, I am pleased and proud to report that when he left his state school he had gained 9 GCSE's , 4 at 'C' and above, one being an 'A' in Drama. This year he passed a BTEC National Diploma in Lesiure Studies, having achieved several merits within the course.

When asked if I wished to make a contribution to this book about dyslexia and stress, my first thought was to write about the stress suffered by not having been diagnosed dyslexic, but felt it was not quite what the editors had in mind. I have decided to give focus to the stress in my working life which is the direct result of being dyslexic.

Dyslexic stress in my working life

Minute-taking

The organisation that I work for has no regular minute taker, which means in certain situations such as reviews it falls to me to take the minutes if no one else is prepared to do so. In such situations I find it difficult to be sellective about what is being discussed. This can result in choosing between two different stratagies:

a) being selective and loosing some of the discussion
b) trying to write down every thing word for word and attempting to sort out the jumbled mess of unformed incomplete words straight afer the meeting to produce something realiable and readable for the typist.

Which ever course of action I choose it is anxiety and stress provoking above that of non dyslexics.

Report writing/exams

Like most dyslexics I use a 'dual track' thought process when writing:

a) the creative ideas of what I wish to say
b) listening in my mind to the sounds the words that I wish to use are making to enable the reader (my self included) to be able to raed and understand the finished product.

After such periods of prolonged concentrated writing I aways experience the feelings of mental and physical fatigue and painful headaches. As we know from studies of stress (Coleman, 1988; Patel, 1988) that stress can cause physical 'unwell' symptoms.

Meeting/case conferences

There are two problems in relation to my dyslexia which present as a problem in such situations:

a) if people talk too fast I can miss some of the debate
b) difficulty of holding on to an idea in my short-term memory that I wish to use as a personal contribution to the debate, if when the idea presents it's self I do not do something with it it can become lost forever.

With regards to 'b' I have two possible courses of action open to me. Firstly, I could result to 'butting-in' with my idea. This can (and quite rightly) be viewed as being inpolite and even antagonise other people, especially the person being interupted. It looks and feels unprofesional which again is stress proving. Added to which if someone makes a derogatory statement about such behaviour it futher adds to the anxiety and stress. Secondly, one can employ the strategy of writing the idea down as it comes to mind. Again to be able to do this a dual thought process is required which results in missing some of the debate while writing all of which adds to the stress level.

I could take the easy less stressful option and let my contribution be lost, but, that would result in feeling of frustration and inadaquacy and of a feeling of not doing my job as well as I am capable of. For dyslexics in a professional setting there is no way of avoiding stress since they cannot afford to take the easy path, we always have to walk the bumpy road in ill fitting shoes. By the very nature of our dyslexia we will suffer more stress in such situations as described. The fact that the dyslexia handicap is hidden to view from others actualy only compounds the stress suffered.

Where does the stress come from?

My experience of stress comes from several aspects:

a) feeling inadaquate and frustrated with my own mental/brain processes
b) frustrated by the hiddeness of the handicap, of other peoples lack of knowledge and understanding of what I am struggling to cope with
c) finding such situations as out-linned previous, anxiety provoking.

Of all the aspects that are anxiety and stress provoking it is the inter-link of the hidenness of the handicape and a bad dyslexia day that I personally find psychologically and physically stressful.

I am currently employed as a General Manager of four small group homes (three people in each home) for young adults with border-line learning and emotional needs. What follows is an example of the start of a bad dyslexic day.

Disruptive cycle of dyslexia

I recently went into a shop to purchase a household item for one of the group homes that needed to be delivered by the stores transport. The assistant ask for the address of where it was to be delivered, a simple enough question for some one who goes regularly to the address, that is only the case if you are not dyslexic and having one of those dyslexic days. I first gave her the name and number of the wrong house, quickly tried to correct the position, but I could see clouds of doubt crossing her forehead. On the second attempt I got the house name and road correct, but as soon as the number had crossed my lips I began to have doubts that this was correct. I took a deep breath and told her I think the number was wrong, but I could not remember if it was 108 or 109, she was not a happy lady I could see the storm clouds gathering. In an attempt to get it right the next time round, I ask permission to phone the house concerned to check the house number. On using the phone I misdialed (didgets in wrong order), I made my apologies to the unknown person on the other end of the line, in full view of a by now quite confussed sales assistent. On my second attempt I got through to the correct number and ask the care officer on duty for the house number, she expressed some surprise and I could hear her chuckling to her self as I replaced the phone. On completion of the sale, when I was about to leave the shop I ask the sales assistant for the receipt, saying she had not given it to me. She was adamant that she had and prompted me to search my bag, whereupon I found it in a side pocket, I had no recolection of her giving it to me, or of my own actions. The non verbal interaction which I could see taking place between the sales assistent and her colleague did little to help my self-esteem. I reminded my self I was not stupid, just dyslexic and that I had tomorrow to look forward to, and that with luck my mental processes might be more 'conformists', since past experiences told me that this was just the beginning of a disruptive dyslexic day.

I would like to say that such an occassion as discribed is rare that it happened at the end of a particulary busy day. This was not the case, it was my first task of my working day and the beggining of the week. It was one of those unexplained days when my dyslexia makes it's self known to the outside world in a 'mega-phone' way. I don't know why I have days like this. At such times I can be particullary clumsy, knocking into things, walking into door frames, spilling drinks etc. Two months ago I had a very stressful experience; when in a large DIY shop purchasing tins of household paint, I don't know how I misjudged the lifting of a very large tin of paint from it's shelf, but suddenly other paint fell to the floor landing on my foot and bursting. I was not a pretty sight – knee deep in paint unable to see my shoes or legs. I was quickly ussered away by several staff to start the ardous task of cleaning me up, on such occassions hand blow dryers can come in very useful for drying cloths. To say that the staff were kind to me is an understatement. I can say that I would feel anxious about buying paint again .

If I had not been aware of my dyslexia I would begin to suspect some kind of brain disorder starting to show. Such disruptive days are compounded by the fact that when experiencing it, I desperately want to use some kind of adjustments or strategies to get some kind of balance. I don't know if the awareness creates an unerlying anxiety which in turn set up a cycle of disruption, but I do know that such times are very stress provoking. I see the disruption cycle as follows:

a) poor coordination
b) information accessing problems
c) loss of confidence to produce the correct information
d) lowering of self-esteem
e) increased anxiety
f) feeling stressed
g) experiencing the physical symptoms of stress (such as headache).

For me personally I don't experience an isolated 'black-spot', if it's a bad day it's a bad day, like riding a storm, just hang in and try to get through the day with out too many problems.

Physical stress

Due to poor coordination in an attempt to aid my letter formation I have always held my pen over tight, as with typing (I have been teaching my self to type) I press the keys too heavy. I have been experiencing tendon problems with my writing hand and wrist. I have worn a brace on it and recieved hospital treatment of injection. This did relieve the problems for some months but is beginning to return as a problem.

Unconsicence baggage

I find that my early educational experience come back to haunt me on bad days. When experiencing a problem especially if coments are made by observers I can at times experience a kind of emotional flash-back of particulary painful and fearful classroom experiences. Things that I had no previous memory of. I well understand the need for dyslexics to grow a tough hide, but I also feel that for people whose early school life was so traumatic there is a need for this to be addressed at some point, since it is more healthy to have emotional baggage 'cleaned and tieded'. For me personally I dont' feel angrey at the loss of my educational right, when I think about it I feel I sadness at the loss. Could any of this unconcious trauma get in the way of things on a bad dyslexia day?

References

Coleman V (1988). *Stress Management Techniques*. London: Gold Arrow Publication.
Patel C (1988). *Understanding Stress*. London: Hodder & Stoughton.
Miles TR (1978). *Understanding Dyslexia*. London: Hodder & Stoughton

Brother Matthew Sasse: The positive and the negative

People often say to me: 'I *sometimes* forget people's names but usually don't find it a problem'. If it happened only *occasionally* to me, I would find it easier to laugh it off. But it has happened *too* frequently in the past and caused me great embarrassment, so I am at great pains to avoid that situation by following detailed strategies, like writing out a list before I go to a meeting with people I have not seen for some time, and having that list easily accessible in my pocket. This is just one instance of how my dyslexia puts pressure on me.

Dyslexia means, in my case, lack of organisation. My room tends to look like a bombsite. Yet I know where everything is, because it's not all filed neatly away but is all on view so that I can put my hands on it quickly. This habit has its drawbacks however because if I need to cross the room at speed, that's not always possible! Then I'm inclined to get angry with myself because I am keeping people waiting. Also if anyone opens the door, the room looks somewhat intimidating, especially as they can't usually sit down because the armchair is covered with books and papers.

Being right-brained means that I know intuitively how things work which is not always welcome, for instance if I manage to start a car first go after somebody else has nearly drained the battery in their efforts to get it started. It might be more tactful not to intervene! It can also be frustrating for others that I dislike reading through operation manuals or leaflets from cover to cover but prefer to 'dive' right in and follow my instinct. This is particularly true when adjusting or mending digital watches. I prefer to experiment until I have worked out how they function; it is usually quicker!

They say that schooldays should be the happiest days of your life; that was certainly not true in my case. It was not a total nightmare but I soon learned to take precautions. Precise strategies were quickly evolved and a standard set of excuses were trundled out on a regular basis. The best, undetectable avoidance strategy was a serious stomach ache fifteen minutes before I had to leave for school.

It was necessary to plan ahead where I would sit for the lessons where I always had difficulty, however hard I tried. The best place was out to the side near the back where I was not in the teacher's direct line of sight. But I had no solution to FRENCH DICTATION! I always scored nought out of ten, or even minus marks, which never failed to aggravate the teacher who was a Frenchman himself. He seemed to take it as an insult both to his home country and to his teaching ability. As so many dyslexics find, after a point, the harder you try, the worse it seems to get. I often ended up in tears! While trying to correct errors I just spelt differently but still not correctly. It wasn't only the teacher who became frustrated!

It was at university when the pressures of my dyslexic difficulties very nearly brought me to my knees. I could not keep up with the essays. The thought of everything resting on a week of final exams after three years' work became intolerable. In one term I had lost a stone and a half in weight, the doctor suggested tranquillisers and I was about to ask, for a third time, not to complete the course. Luckily I found a senior tutor who managed to convince me that, as I had survived till now, the university authorities must consider I was worthy of a degree, so it was just a question of persevering to the end. The stress that I suffered then was the worst I have ever experienced.

Writing letters has never come easily to me. As a child I needed plenty of persuasion to write Christmas thank-you letters. The final convincing motive was that, if they were not written, I would probably not receive many presents for my birthday in the middle of January. Also it took me over four months before I sat down and faced the task of writing this short article. Frequently I say to friends: 'If you ever receive a letter from me FRAME IT!!!, because you are unlikely to get another one!'

Reading still presents me with a few problems. When reading a newspaper with anyone else in the room usually I find I cannot concentrate. On a 'bad day' I can read a paragraph three times and still not remember the gist of it although I know perfectly well what every word means. On a 'good day' I understand at the first attempt. As I live with a community of religious brothers I am not at liberty to take the newspaper out of the reading room. Result: Frequent Frustration!!

As a child I remember how my father valued education and what he called 'GOOD BOOKS'! Generally it took me twice or three times as long to read a set text for an English exam. or one of Dad's 'GOOD BOOKS'. I learned to dread my father recommending that I read another 'GOOD BOOK'. One of my sayings at that time was: 'I HATE "GOOD BOOKS".' On one occasion the pressure became too much for me. So I put on my black shoes lay, on my bed and kicked up and down the wall leaving great black marks right up the paint-work.

One of the strategies that helps me to live and work effectively is a series of set routines. Each of my pupils has his own personal zip file with always the same eight things in it, like a triangular pencil with a rubber at one end a six-inch ruler with their name on, a notebook for spelling rules, a cardboard file for used work-sheets, etc. As a teacher, even my pencil case has a cardboard partition inside, so I can see at a glance if anything is missing, because I know that on one side are two pens and two pencils and on the other side are five pens or markers.

My briefcase also has a strict layout inside that never varies. The result is that, even if I am in a hurry I can see at a glance whether anything is missing before I close the case and rush out of the room to my next lesson. I go through a set routine of checks before I leave the house so I do not leave things behind.

I learnt the importance of this early on in my working life as an adult. Once I took to the cinema a pencil case with three gold-topped pens in it, which had been a present for my 21st birthday. While I was there, I must have bent down and they must have fallen to the ground. I did not check my pocket before I left the cinema only discovering I had lost them when I returned home. They were never recovered. I was devastated and I could not afford to replace them. It taught me a salutary lesson and nowadays before I leave anywhere I always check my inside pocket to see if my three pens are there. Keeping to these routines all serves to slow me down which means that people may have to wait until

I'm ready, having completed all these checks. Often people become impatient and this is hard for me so sometimes I do not bother. Occasionally I pay the price and forget something like my umbrella, as I did when I dashed away from a British Dyslexia Association meeting last year.

Dyslexia does have a positive side to it. I'm sure it's made me a more efficient problem solver. When others are, at first, 'stumped' when presented with a *new problem* I can 'dive' straight in and apply a series of possible solutions until I find one that works. Problem solved! Life for this dyslexic can present a series of difficulties due to short-term memory, poor concentration, etc. which may be stressful but occasionally quite rewarding, as when you arrive at a novel solution to a problem which no one else has thought of like my word index that was published in the latest edition of *Alpha to Omega* by Beve Hornsby which should make accessing the spelling rules that much easier.

Sheena Harrison

Dear Tim,

A, by now, very belated reply, hope its not to late for the book. How are you? The tips you gave me have proved to be useful. . .

Now stress and dyslexia, it becomes a permanent companion that swiftly overwhelms at times. My experience is a two layered one, pre knowing and post knowing.

Pre-knowing. I was considered to be a 'highly strung', a b – – – – y nuscience, perhaps a hyperactive child in todays terms, both at home and at school. As being tied to a chair at 3/4 yrs by the teacher – to make me sit still, examples.

At 14/15yrs, I had my appendix taken out, as a last resort, the GP considered I was 'playing my mother up' and my appendix pain was described as being psychosomatic and a result of my nerves at being in the grammer school.

Anxiety and panic were a constant in my childhood, as I lived with the blight of being a scholar with writing, spelling and computational difficulties, not to mention a memory you couldn't rely on. My mother, a nurse, used to consider I needed medication to 'calm me down' and intermitently, make me go to sleep, especially at exam times and for the 11+ exam.

Anxiety overwhelmed me at exam time. In the 2nd year Juniors I rember being only able to put my name on the page. Similarly at the 'O' Level exams, I achieved 2 'O' Levels passes – History and RE. Work to was to prove to be a nightmare of waiting to be found out to be an incompetent.

I have suffered with day time stress incontinence since early school days. It remains to this day a problem that continues to puzzle medical professionals and yet again my symptoms do not fit their 'normal' typologies. I don't own up to this aspect of stress to many Tim. I bit my nails to as a child and today bite the skin around my nails.

I personally believe today that the overwhelming levels of anxiety created by the daily ignominies and embarrassments of being a dyslexic person functioning in society, fuelled my abusing myself with prescribed medication and alcohol. The verbal beratings for unexplainable errors to parents, teachers and peers, the constant 'showing ups' in shops, on public transport and in other public situations as the dyslexic dysfunctioning outed eroded my self-worth and self-esteem. A psychatrist once described me as having a 'slight' inferiority complex.

I was prescribed Valium a number of times, as a treatment for my dry scalp which my GP considered was attributule to stress. When I stop awhile and reflect, I have been offered treatments for conditions that have been ascribed to stress most of life, by the medical profession.

Eventually, despite medication, GPs' prescribed to relieve anxiety, I turned to alcohol to anaesthetise the resultant levels of anxiety. I used alcohol Tim for fifteen years to 'help' me deal with life people and social interactions, in ignorance of the dyslexia and dyscalcula that flaws my daily social functioning's.

Post knowing, at 45 years of age, that I was a person with both dyslexia and dyscalcula. Uncovered at Bangor University by the specialist help made available at the Dyslexic Unit, I was to discover the levels of stress that being involved and exposure in education produced in myself and preversely being a belated academic success. I sought counselling and was given 'Beta Blockers' by my GP who, when I presented myself when the 'panic attacks' and the resultant fibrillation's, were beginning to be a daily trail, in my first year.

His comment was 'what do you expect as a dyslexic Sheena' as I expressed my puzzlement at him considering I needed this type of medication. Despite not wanting to take medication, the daily poundings of 'abnormal' stress levels forced me to considering the 'docs' advice, relief followed as the cycle of panic attacks were reduced. At least till exam times.

Today I have an awareness of the holistic persuasiveness, the affects and effects of having dyslexia compounded by having dyscalcula. This has enabled me to develop a range of strategies for dealing and coping with my levels of stress. It still catches me out when I get over tired or anxious about me in work and educational situations. I am at present receiving counselling and have had to 'look at' the effects of being a person with dyslexia and dyscalcula and their impact on my life. I have recently worked with a group of Post Truamatic Stress Disordered ex-service personnel and have observed the extreme effects of long term truamatisation. The similarities have struck me, although I realise they are not as extreme for me. The social dysfunctionality also is, in them exaggerated, but nevertheless comparable to my own experiences and those I have known with other dyslexics. I am working with one at present who has been severly afflicted socially & functionally since adolescence. She is almost like the 'wolfe child' – been locked away and not been allowed to have a normal adolescence. Kieth – – – has done the testing & she has proved to be severely dyslexic & dysculic.

Lots of caring thoughts and special heartfelt thanks for your work and concern for advancing knowledge.

Sheena

Janet Coker

I am a singer. before all els I am a singer, my hole being sings. I am also a wife a mother gardener, window cleaner, cooke house cleaner, painter decorateor, you name it I will have a go.

I am a diselexeix I am a diselexic singer, wife mother gardener ect, ect.

Being diselexicc has maid me at time's very angry very frustrated and has resulted in countless humileations. You eather go under or become stronger with each ocation. Laughter is a great healer I have red and said some helarious things quite serilesey, lurn to laugh at yourself and outhers will laugh with you and not at you.

When I was a little girl I was concidered very backward I could not read or spell or write legilbeey, but I could sing, I would go into the lockel woods and filds and sing my hart out.

If the music is growing out of your sole, you cant stope it. Do not get stuck behind dots on paper words you cant reed. Make sounds, thrilling vibrations, take of into the realmes of your own emagination blow your horn, strum your gitar, crash your cords or cress each note of your piano

The pure joy of making music be it with voice or insterament is with out limit. make music go for it sweep aside barriers buld your own bridges

I am a singer before all els I am a singer

Chapter 10
An overview

TIM MILES and VED VARMA

Although there is reason to think that awareness of the needs of dyslexic children and adults has become very much more widespread in the last 10–15 years, it is still possible for a parent to have a horrendous time in seeking help. This is made very clear by Karen Dodd in Chapter 1: her attempts on behalf of Margaret appear to have met with responses that were not merely unsympathetic but actively hostile. It is these responses that she describes as 'the attitude'; and it is clear that for those who encounter it 'the attitude' is a major source of stress.

The remedy, as Angela Fawcett points out in Chapter 2, rests primarily with those responsible for the training of teachers. One frequently meets the objection that there is no space in a crowded teacher-training syllabus to add anything further, but one cannot help wondering if those who argue in this way are showing the right sense of priorities. There may also still be a few educational psychologists who are far from blameless, and again this is something that needs to be taken on board by those who train them. We of course do not believe that there is any significant number of individuals who would deliberately set out to be unkind, but, even so, there may sometimes be lapses from suitable standards of professionalism. One of the key requirements for anyone who enters the 'helping' professions is to be a good listener, and if after a discussion with a parent one is left with the feeling that that parent is dissatisfied, one is failing in one's professional duty if one does not try harder to discover the reasons. Professionals may sometimes secretly feel that the parent is being unnecessarily 'difficult', but in that case the correct procedure is to find out more as to why that parent is behaving in that particular way and what earlier provocations led to it. The same is of course true when one deals with a 'difficult' child – as is shown at the end of Chapter 3 where Patience Thomson describes how she dealt with a 10-year-old boy who had kicked one of his schoolmates! Perhaps one may even come to doubt whether 'being difficult' is an appropriate way of talking about the situation. It is very easy, too, for a teacher or educational psychologist to feel threatened when parents say that their child is dyslexic – and then to take refuge in pretending to be more sure about that child's needs than they actually are. Similarly, if professionals are tempted to dismiss a parent's calls for help on the grounds that that parent is 'over-anxious', it is important to remember that it is not the job of the professional to be 'judgemental'. That a parent is anxious may not be in dispute – but by what right can one say that that parent is *over*-anxious? This is to sit in judgement when the true role of the professional is to try to understand.

The issue is one that has ramifications far beyond the area of dyslexia. An important question that should be asked in any training course is 'What is the cost of being wrong?'. To allow someone to feel that they are over-anxious when it would be more correct to say that they are justifiably anxious is an appalling kind of error, comparable, perhaps, to allowing the parents of a schizophrenic teenager to believe that it is their behaviour that has caused the schizophrenia or to accusing an innocent person that he has sexually abused his child. Similarly, even the most sceptical professionals should ask themselves, 'What if the mother who assures me that her child is dyslexic is right after all? Have I really examined the most recent scientific evidence in sufficient detail to be sure that she is wrong?'. At the very least it would be right to give her the opportunity to explain why she has this belief and what it all means to her.

Finally, if the problem is really shortage of time or resources then it is dishonest to use this as a reason for denying the dyslexia. What doctor would tolerate being told not to diagnose a condition because resources were not available for treating it? There is no reason why teachers or educational psychologists should think of themselves any differently.

A theme that occurs in virtually all the chapters is that of the stress caused by having to take examinations or undergo 'appraisal'; particularly noteworthy in this connection are the appalling stresses undergone by Sheena Harrison (as described in Chapter 9). Moreover it was in a test situation that Margaret Dodd finally lost control (Chapter 1), whereas it was the statement that she would 'never pass an exam' that caused Claire Newby to throw ink over her teacher (Chapter 9)! In view of the pressure that current methods of examining place on dyslexics we should perhaps be surprised by the fact that such outbursts are relatively infrequent.

An examination, after all, is an invitation to prove one's worth and which of us does not wish to be 'worth' something? Yet dyslexics are being asked to prove their worth via a medium – the written word – which, for them, makes such proof extra difficult. Peter Congdon refers in Chapter 7 to dyslexics who refuse to accept special provision in examinations because this seems like receiving favoured treatment. However, there is no suggestion of favouritism if examination boards make it their business to ensure that candidates are not penalised for lack of skills that are irrelevant to the subject of the examination. For example, it is arguable that there is no particular merit in requiring people to be able to write at speed or to remember a long list of names which thereafter they will easily be able to look up in a book.

We should like to mention in this connection the stresses experienced by some dyslexics when they take examinations in music. For example, a dyslexic who has achieved genuine competence in playing scales on the piano may suddenly be confronted in an examination with the rapidly spoken instruction, 'B minor, left hand, three octaves'.* This may be too much for him to 'take in' or the effort involved in having to understand the spoken words may lead him to play worse than he otherwise would have done.

It is to the credit of the musical profession that steps are now being taken to alert examiners to the needs of the dyslexic. The advice that is being prepared runs as follows:†

- Relevant potential difficulties for a dyslexic candidate.
- The nervousness which anyone may have at an examination is likely to be intensified for a dyslexic candidate because of the fear that he or she may 'make a fool of themselves' – caused by (apparently) 'stupid mistakes'.
- *Aim* to convey the impression that there is *plenty* of *time and space*: no one is being rushed; you will not be surprised by anything that happens – you are prepared for it.
- *Avoid* any kind of 'talking down' to the candidate or 'poor old chap' (either of these kinds of sympathy are *not* wanted!)

Then follows some advice about the possible need to repeat instructions (because a dyslexic candidate may easily become confused or forget them), about the need to speak slowly, and about giving candidates a second chance if they lose their way, for instance, by forgetting what scale they are playing. The important thing is that, if examiners bear these suggestions in mind, then the examinee is being afforded a proper chance to display what he can do and is not being penalised for lack of skills that are irrelevant to what is being examined. (For further discussion of the problems facing examining boards see Gilroy and Miles, 1995, Chapter 8.)

Perhaps even more significant are the social stresses to which dyslexics are exposed. In one form or another all the contributors emphasise this. In this connection, as both Patience Thomson points out in Chapter 3 and Michael Newby in Chapter 9, we need to remember that these

---

*We owe this example to Caroline Beaumont, who is a member of the British Dyslexia Association Working Party on Dyslexia and Music.
†We are grateful to Margaret Hubicki, also a member of the above Working Party, for permission to quote these instructions.

stresses can occur before the time when difficulty with reading or spelling begins to show itself. Thus a dyslexic child may forget or misunderstand oral instructions and have to rely on following others, or he may have problems of motor coordination – and in either case this can be very humiliating. All this provides further evidence that if we equate dyslexia simply with 'poor reading' we shall fail to group together the many other characteristics that are regularly found in dyslexics (compare Miles, 1994). Karen Dodd interestingly points out in Chapter 1 that she did not immediately appreciate that Margaret's difficulty in learning to ride a bicycle was in any way connected with her dyslexia. If a diagnosis of dyslexia enables someone to *make sense* of events that at first glance did not seem associated with dyslexia, this in itself can help to reduce stress.

Another source of stress is that dyslexics may often be afraid that they are 'doing the wrong thing'. There is a continual risk of adverse reaction from their peers (Steve Chinn and Maryrose Crossman, Chapter 4); they may not make friends easily (Patience Thomson, Chapter 3) or become withdrawn or solitary (Dorothy Gilroy, Chapter 5); and their lack of confidence may be particularly exposed when they apply for jobs or when their work has to be appraised (Gerald Hales, Chapter 6). In this connection Patience Thomson draws an analogy with the situation that many non-dyslexics have experienced – that of trying to find their way in a foreign town when they have little or no knowledge of the native language.

Roger Saunders has aptly reminded us, in Chapter 8, of the many subtle interactions that can exist within the family. Particularly moving is the reported parental comment, 'Thank goodness, we've got our little boy back'. This is something that can regularly happen when a child, as a result of increasing frustration, has become totally discouraged and has 'withdrawn into his shell' – and then receives the kind of help that enables him once more to be the cheerful person which he originally was. Roger also reminds us of the appalling harm which can be done if untrained teachers 'continue to "pound away" at teaching strategies which are *inappropriate*'. What he tellingly calls 'academic abuse' can be at least as damaging as physical abuse.

There are many other subtle social reactions. According to Angela Fawcett (Chapter 2), Dominic showed behaviour problems 'as a smoke screen to hide the fact that he cannot cope'. There is also the response mentioned by Steve Chinn and Maryrose Crossman (Chapter 4): 'if I think I am going to fail then I won't do my best so when I do fail I can think, "Well, I didn't try".'

What emerges in particular from all this is the need for an efficient system of counselling. This applies in particular in the case of teenage and adult dyslexics (see especially Chapters 4, 5 and 6). Lessons in social skills – they need not be formal ones – can clearly be of considerable help, as can help with reading 'body language'. If dyslexics are trained to *notice* small bodily movements and the like they will have a better sense of what others are thinking. As a result they will be less likely to commit social 'gaffes': they may recognise, for example, from their hearer's facial expression that what they are saying is not going down very well, or from their hostess's fidgeting that they have outstayed their welcome at a supper party! These things may seem trivial in themselves, but consistent failure to 'read the signs' may lead to strained relations and a cycle of misunderstandings. Tolerance on the part of others is, of course, essential.

Angela Fawcett, Dorothy Gilroy, Peter Congdon and Michael Newby all refer to *In the Mind's Eye* (West, 1991). One of the important consequences of this book is that it encourages us all to think *positively* about dyslexia – to focus our attention on what dyslexics *can* do rather than on what they *cannot* do. West's biographical sketches indicate that many successful thinkers have had an unusual balance of skills – high creative ability in spite of late reading or a poor school record; his work is therefore of particular value to those dyslexics who are inclined to be diffident about their own abilities. As he rightly points out, many of the operations which dyslexics find difficult are of a 'clerical' kind and in the present age can therefore be carried out by computer. This means that they are left free to develop their talents without being too much handicapped by their relative weaknesses in literacy.

One of the most serious consequences of academic failure and social uncertainty is a loss of self-esteem. It is plain from the various case studies reported throughout the book that the happiest dyslexics were those who were able to make full use of their abilities. Even then, however, we should not forget that dyslexics are *vulnerable*, and it is noteworthy that even someone as successful as Susan Hampshire should nevertheless have had the really stressful experience which she describes in the Foreword.

Finally, there are a few points, among the many interesting ones made by the contributors, which we should like to single out for special mention.

Angela Fawcett has pointed out in Chapter 2 how easy it is to assume – wrongly – that because a dyslexic can function well in one situation he will necessarily be able to function well in another – perhaps a seemingly similar one but in important respects different. For example, it is much easier to produce the correct spelling of a word in a one-to-one situation with a sympathetic teacher than to have to spell the same word in an examination or in the hurly-burly of the classroom. Angela has also called attention to the fact that for physiological reasons dyslexics may have fewer resources to bring to bear on a particular problem, and to achieve the desired result may therefore have to put in an extra large amount of effort. Not surprisingly, therefore, they tire easily, as is also pointed out by Patience Thomson (Chapter 3), Dorothy Gilroy (Chapter 5), Gerald Hales (Chapter 6) and Joy Aldridge (Chapter 9). It often happens, too, that if they try harder things get worse rather than better (Brother Matthew, Chapter 9). Feelings of dismay may also occur if they see their peers completing written work with effortless ease whereas they themselves have to struggle for many hours. Both Dorothy Gilroy (Chapter 5) and Peter Congdon (Chapter 7) point out that there are some dyslexics who feel a strong sense of injustice. Herodotus (*Histories*, Book vii, section 152) says that if everyone's troubles were put in a 'pool' most of us would be happy to take away our own rather than run the risk of having to endure those of someone else. There may be truth in this, but we cannot but sympathise with those dyslexics who sometimes feel within themselves, 'It's all so *unfair*'.

It is a matter of familiar experience that tension in any situation can often be defused by laughter. This is certainly true where such tension is the consequence of dyslexia. The temptation to say to a dyslexic in an exasperated voice, 'I *told* you; why didn't you listen?', becomes less when one remembers the difficulty which dyslexics experience in understanding verbal instructions and can therefore laugh at the situation. I remember being totally exasperated some years ago when a 13-year-old dyslexic girl was about an hour late for her lesson with one of my colleagues on two consecutive occasions, and it was particularly maddening because her parents could not afford to pay and precious 'hardship' funds were being used to finance her. It was only at the time of the third lesson that I was able to see the funny side – she turned up over an hour early. Then the penny dropped, and I suggested to her teacher that what the girl needed was instruction in the use of a watch!

The recognition that it is important to be able to laugh is present, at least implicitly, in many of the contributions. Brother Matthew in Chapter 9 has some uncomplimentary things to say about the state of his desk – but he is able to be light-hearted about the matter! Similarly Angela Fawcett in Chapter 2 is able – at least in retrospect – to be light-hearted about the situation when the other Matthew (her son) left some sausages burning and set fire to the house. Janet Coker (in Chapter 9) explicitly mentions the part that can be played by laughter in easing tension, though she rightly emphasises that we must laugh with dyslexics and not at them.

To sum up. If stress among dyslexics and their families is to be lessened the following appear to be some of the main requirements:

1. All teachers and educational psychologists during their training should be alerted to the needs of the dyslexic child.
2. Our examination system should be organised in such a way that dyslexics are given a proper chance to show their abilities and are not

penalised by lack of skills which are irrelevant to the purpose of the examination.

3. People should be alerted to the fact that dyslexics can sometimes be deficient in social skills – for example, in keeping appointments or in their ability to 'read' people's feelings. This is a consequence of the dyslexia and not something that one should 'wax indignant' about.
4. There should be a greater emphasis on the talents of dyslexics.
5. Whatever their struggles over achieving literacy they should never be allowed to lose their self-respect.

References

Miles TR (1994). A proposed taxonomy and some consequences. In Fawcett AJ, Nicolson RI (Eds), *Dyslexia in Children: Multidisciplinary Perspectives*. London: Harvester Wheatsheaf.

Gilroy DE, Miles TR (1995). *Dyslexia at College*, 2nd edn. London: Routledge.

West TG (1991). *In the Mind's Eye*. Buffalo, NY: Prometheus Books.

Subject index

academic abuse 101, 122
ACID profile (on Wechsler test) 90
ADO (Adult Dyslexia organisation) 106
Annals of Dyslexia 102
autism 13, 107
automaticity 24–27
balancing 24–29
Bangor Dyslexia Test 23
Bartholemews, *see* St Bartholemews Hospital
bed wetting 41, 42
body image 38
body language 37, 50, 53, 64, 123
brain organisation 14, 23, 90, 113
British Dyslexia Association xiii, 100
cerebellum, role of, 28
clumsiness 10, 11, 17, 19, 24, 38, 39, 111
concentration problems 41
confusion, see under 'spatial awareness' and 'temporal awareness'
conscious concentration hypothesis 25
Connor's Behavioural Questionnaire 13
creativity 100
DAD (dyslexia automation deficit) hypothesis 25
delinquency 54, 93, 94
diagnosis (sc. of dyslexia), effects of, 2, 5, 6, 12, 94, 101,115, 116
Disabled Students' Allowance 56, 65
Dunedin epidemiological study 13, 14
dyslexia
    hereditary component in, 15, 23
    hostility to the concept vii, 1–3, 107,
    whether to use the label 11, 12
Dyslexia Institute 16, 17, 19

dyslexic employees 87
dyspraxia, *see* clumsiness.
examinations 46, 50, 61, 70, 84, 94, 95, 120, 124 (*see also* music examinations)
expressive language 37
eye contact 53
family history 1, 14, 16, 18, 21, 98, 105, 106 (*see also* heredity)
form filling v (*see also* job applications)
'good' and 'bad' days 31, 62, 110, 114
heredity, 15, 23, 100
humour, role of, 70, 117, 124
hygiene (personal) 51
interviews 76–79
job applications 74–76, 122
Kershaw Report 86
laughter, *see* humour
left-right confusion 38
malsequencing 106
mathematical difficulties 34, 35, 42, 69, 105, 106, 116
'Matthew' effect 12, 31
memorising difficulties 7, 8, 9, 11, 17, 35, 36, 109, 115, 121, 122
motor skills, weakness in, 36, 38
music examinations 121
Open University 108
Orton Dyslexia Society 103
panic v
parental pressures 14, 51, 91
phonological deficits 23, 27, 28, 29, 35, 37
poetry, writing of, 66, 106
promotion 83–85
psychiatric diagnoses 14

127

Author index

129